To Linda
 I've enjoyed getting to know you during the past few years at the family gathering. I pray this book blesses you.

 Rhonda

Journey Of Love

Rhonda Sanders

Bloomington, IN   Milton Keynes, UK
authorHOUSE®

AuthorHouse™
1663 Liberty Drive, Suite 200
Bloomington, IN 47403
www.authorhouse.com
Phone: 1-800-839-8640

AuthorHouse™ UK Ltd.
500 Avebury Boulevard
Central Milton Keynes, MK9 2BE
www.authorhouse.co.uk
Phone: 08001974150

© *2006 Rhonda Sanders. All rights reserved.*

No part of this book may be reproduced, stored in a retrieval system, or transmitted by any means without the written permission of the author.

First published by AuthorHouse 11/16/2006

ISBN: 978-1-4259-6697-3 (sc)
ISBN: 978-1-4259-6698-0 (hc)

Library of Congress Control Number: 2006908455

Printed in the United States of America
Bloomington, Indiana

This book is printed on acid-free paper.

The many ways that God has had his hand on me and my family is just amazing! We truly do have so much to be thankful for, and believe me when I say, I AM so very thankful for His many blessings on us and to us!

I am a single mother, married and divorced four, yes, four times! My children are the most precious gifts that I feel God has temporarily given to me to care for - I say, "temporarily" because, ultimately I know that they belong to Him just as I belong to Him.

I have two sons and one daughter and I must say that God truly knew what He was doing placing these three beautiful individuals in my life. And, they ARE very unique individuals - each one different in personality type and attitudes! Each one of them has taught me different life lessons and I am grateful to them and for them. We have been through some very adverse times, yet the joys outweigh the adversity and I am so glad they were there with me to share these joyful times, knowing that they also learned some things to help them survive the future.

This book is a part of my testimony.

Table of Contents

Chapter One
    THE JOURNEY BEGINS   1

Chapter Two
    JOURNEY OF THE WORD   11

Chapter Three
    JOURNEY OF PRAISE   19

Chapter Four
    JOURNEY OF THANKFULNESS   33

Chapter Five
    JOURNEY OF FORGIVENESS   41

Chapter Six
    JOURNEY OF FAITH   57

Chapter Seven
    JOURNEY OF OBEDIENCE   65

Chapter Eight
    JOURNEY OF INTERCESSION   71

Chapter Nine
    JOURNEY OF PEACE   79

Chapter Ten
    JOURNEY OF PURPOSE   85

Chapter Eleven
    JOURNEY OF LOVE   91

Chapter One
The Journey Begins

My name is Rhonda and I am a single mom of three children. (They are all teens now, so they hate the word "children.")

When I was growing up, I occasionally heard about other children who were raised in a different lifestyle, but never really saw much of any lifestyle except attending church on a regular basis, which meant being there every time the doors were open, because my parents were both Christians and active in the denominational church that we attended. We stayed so busy with church activities and meetings that I really didn't take the time to note other lifestyles.

I can remember taking homework to church. Homework was not an excuse to miss church services. No excuses were acceptable! And, I don't remember wanting to miss too much, all of our friends and closest family members were always there. It was a pretty close-knit group and I grew up thinking that everyone had that "cushion" in their own church lives. I thought everyone lived like that until I became a teenager.

My mother was very talented with the sewing machine and we were always dressed nicely. My father was the manager of a local chain grocery store for most of my earlier school years and later went to work for a carbon black company in our hometown, working his way up to a supervisory position and continued to work there until he retired.

When we were younger, my mother worked "part-time" at a fast food "drive-in" for several years. "Part-time" was at least 40 hours a week! Then she went to work at a sewing factory, also working her way up to a supervisor's position, a job that she retired from.

I think that my sister and I both thought we must have been rich, because it seemed we never did lack. If we did lack anything, we didn't know it and I cannot remember it! We seemed to be pretty well provided for and our family was pretty happy and content with our lives, as well as always busy doing something at school or church. My sister and I both had a short session of piano lessons and participated in the various school activities that we chose. We had even convinced some of our friends at school and church that we were rich, until they came to visit our home and realized that we were no richer than they were! We had a well furnished, modest sized home and since there were only the two of us children, it was quite comfortable. I know my mother was always working on buying something new for the house - saving and putting things on layaway.

We were probably what most people today would consider "sheltered", but we had a very good life. I know that now, especially since I have met so many different people from different lifestyles and different histories and heard the stories of some of their lives. But, even though I had accepted Jesus into my heart as a young girl of eight, I somehow forgot that God was the one who was in control of my life and I began to rebel against Him and my "religious" background gradually, not like my peers, during my teen years. No, I waited until I had already been married to my first husband for a while before I began to notice that people really did live different lifestyles from us and decided to try out some of their lifestyles for myself.

I continued to attend church, because, of course, that is what you did, right? But, the other lifestyles of partying and drinking and overspending and selfish thinking and acts were very appealing to me and I began to be drawn in by Satan to experiment - just a little going out with a friend after work for a drink or meeting an old friend for a drink, just a little of this and that, and continuing to try to maintain that facade that a lot of Christians present to the world. But, guess what! Anyone who had any contact with me on a regular basis KNEW that I was not even trying to live for Jesus or walk with His guidance in my life.

I even at one time was part of a "gospel singing group" and we traveled on a limited basis, singing at various denominational churches in our area of West Texas and New Mexico. However, I still did not truly have a relationship with God, Jesus, or the Holy Spirit! I taught Sunday School, taught the Missionettes - a young girls group, played piano as needed, sang in church choirs, led a children's choir at one time and none of those "works" induced me to draw closer to God.

When I allowed myself to get to the point of a divorce with my first husband, this did not put up the red flag to me that something was wrong with my life. I just kept on doing my own thing (plowing my own field) and with a very young son, decided to re-marry almost immediately. God was not consulted in this decision, because, hey, I could take care of myself! God was so gracious to me, though, because He continued to bless me even during this marriage. He blessed me with a daughter and another son.

God's hand was even on my life when I was not trying to walk with him during this time. Before my last child was born, I had been told not to worry about birth control because there was no way I would be able to have any more children, that my womb was turned the wrong way and it would not be possible for me to conceive another child. I have to tell you that men don't know everything! I did conceive another child, with whom I had a very normal, healthy pregnancy and birth with no complications, and this child was very healthy, as well. God loved me enough that even though I wasn't paying Him any attention other than attending church, He gave me these other two blessings!

When my marriage to this husband did not work out and ended in another divorce, I still did not completely turn my life over to God - quite the opposite. I was so stubborn and determined that I could do everything myself, working and supporting my children during the day and partying with friends almost every night. It was through partying that I met my third husband, who moved in with us during the first week of our acquaintance! Yes, I made many stupid mistakes, but the amazing thing that I want you to see is just HOW MUCH God loved me even then! In the midst of my stubbornness, God continued to bless me and love on me. I lived with this man for several months without being married and eventually moved with him and my three children to another city, where we did get married. Within a few weeks of marriage, though, I was praying for God to get him out of our lives. This was when various types of abuse began.

God did answer my prayers. After three years in a very abusive and controlling relationship with me feeling guilty and resentful of God for allowing me to get into this position (like I had nothing to do with getting there, does this sound familiar to you?) God finally did release me from that horrible experience, but not before my children and I all went through a period of living "hell" on earth. We all make decisions that we have to live with, and I want to remind you that there are principals set up in the Bible, one that applied at that time was the one of reaping what I sowed. God still had His hand on our lives. It was during this period of time that my oldest son chose to go and live with his biological father, and even though it really hurt me at the time, I elected to allow him to make this decision for himself and sent him to live with his father. I thank God now that I made that decision, knowing now what I do that I wasn't even aware of some things that were happening in my own home at that time. And, now my son is a wonderful young man, more mature in some ways than I could have hoped for or expected!

Yet, even after that most horrific experience, you would think I would have learned to place my faith and trust in God! Stubbornness is not a good thing! I continued to party with friends almost every chance I got. My children and I lived that way for another eighteen months when God chose to bring us back to my hometown. God used my daughter to bring us home. She started to beg me to move back home and finally convinced me to start looking for a job in our hometown. After only a few interviews, God "placed" me at a small Bible-believing non-denominational church as the church's full-time secretary. This was a miracle in itself because I needed a full time position, and prior to my employment, this position was only a part-time job. At that time, I was over qualified for this position, because I was considered a "Professional Secretary", having had many classes and certifications in many different fields including bookkeeping, sign language, computer skills, etc. Again, GOD KNOWS what He's doing. I had a lot of spare time on this job and started doing some pretty extensive research on subjects that interested me in the Bible, such as joy, peace, righteousness, and collected lists of scriptures that applied to those subjects. This was a time in my life when I was able to dedicate a lot of time to studying the Word of God and finding out how it should apply to my life. I was able to do some memorization and a lot of studying self-help books and material. Yet, even then, I still continued to be willful and tried to lead my life through my own selfish desires. I allowed loneliness to dictate to me that I should be married again instead of waiting for God to bring my "husband" to me, I re-married again. I truly thought it would be okay because we were able to discuss the Bible for hours and even agreed on a lot of what we had read. However, this was not the husband that God had chosen for me and even though I attempted to honor him as my husband, was not able to do so. As you can guess, this marriage ended in divorce. If you have been keeping up with the numbers to this point, that was divorce number four!

    At this point, I was ready to give up on men. Good thing, too, because I was needing to renew my vows but not with man at that time, with God. Do you realize that if you haven't renewed your vows to God after walking away from Him the way that I did, He will continue to love, but it may be from a distance? This distance was my own creation, not God's. I had chosen to keep back a part of my heart from being hurt so many times and as a result of the previous abuses, no excuses here, just truth! At this point in my life, I still was very reluctant to give over control of my life to God. And, to be honest with you and myself, I wasn't even sure that I could trust God with my life. So, God allowed me to get into a position where I had no other choice but to trust Him and I even had to go before the Body of Christ in my fellowship and ask for their forgiveness.

Finally! Finally, after 42 years of trying it "My Way", and after having received numerous prophecies and having been a "Bible Christian" for years, it was time to give it all up to Christ. As a "Bible Christian", I was capable of quoting parts of the Bible to someone depending on their needs at that time. I had memorized parts of the Bible and had it in my head, but not in my heart, I knew the Bible - words, but I didn't KNOW the Bible, because I wasn't applying it to my life and taking it to heart and allowing God to speak to me through His Word, the Bible.

At this point in my life, when it became necessary for me to go before my fellowship and confess my sins to them and ask them to forgive me, THAT is what it took for God to bring me "home" to Him. And, now, I am trying to "walk" with Him on a daily basis. I must confess, some days are easier and better than others, but, either way, He's always there and I'd much rather walk with Him than without, good or bad days! Now, I am beginning to understand some of those scriptures that I had memorized, such as "…greater is He that is in me than he that is in the world." (1 John 4:4-5) and "I can do all things through Christ Jesus, who strengthened me…" (Phil. 4:13). There are so many verses I could quote to you that I am just now beginning to walk through with God leading me on this Journey of Love!!

I'd like to share with you the following verses regarding salvation, because, ultimately, my purpose in writing this book is to bring you to the knowledge that Jesus loves you and that He died for you, so please search these verses out for yourself and see that salvation is for YOU!!!

>ROMANS 5:12 - *Wherefore, as by one man sin entered into the world, and death, by sin; and so death passed upon all men, for that all have sinned.*

>ROMANS 3:12 - *For all have sinned, and come short of the glory of God.*

ROMANS 6:23 - *For the wages of sin is death; but the gift of God is eternal life through Jesus Christ our Lord.*

ROMANS 5:8 - *But God commendeth his love toward us, in that, while we were yet sinners, Christ died for us.*

1 CORINTHIANS 15:1-4 - *Moreover, brethren, I declare unto you the gospel which I preached unto you, which also ye have received, and wherein ye stand: By which also ye are saved if ye keep in memory what I preached unto you, unless ye have believed in vain. For I delivered unto you first of all that which I also received, how that Christ died for our sins according to the scriptures; And that He was buried, and that He rose again the third day according to the scriptures.*

JOHN 3:17 - *For God sent not his Son into the world to condemn the world but that the world through Him might be saved.*

JOHN 3:36 - *He that believeth on the Son hath everlasting life; and he that believeth not the Son shall not see life; but the wrath of God abideth on him.*

JOHN 3:16 - *For God so loved the world, that He gave His only begotten Son, that whosoever believeth in Him should not perish, but have everlasting life.*

JOHN 1:12 - *But as many as received Him, to them gave he the power to become the sons of God, even to them that believe on His name;*

EPHESIANS 2:8,9 - *For by grace are ye saved through faith; and that not of yourselves; it is the gift of God. Not of works, lest any man should boast.*

Revelation 3:20 - *Behold, I stand at the door, and knock; if any man hear my voice, and open the door, I will come in to him, and will sup with him, and he with me.*

Romans 10:8-*10 - But what saith it? The word is nigh thee, even in thy mouth, and in thy heart; that is, the word of faith, which we preach; That if thou shalt confess with thy mouth the Lord Jesus, and shalt believe in thine heart that God hath raised Him from the dead, thou shalt be saved. For with the heart man believeth unto righteousness; and with the mouth confession is made unto salvation.*

Matthew 10:32 - *Whosoever therefore shall confess me before men, him will I confess also before my Father which is in heaven.*

1 John 5:11-*13 - And this is the record, that God hath given to us eternal life, and this life is in His Son. He that hath the Son hath life; and he that hath not the Son of God hath no life. These things have I written unt5o you that believe on the name of the Son of God; that ye may know that ye have eternal life, and that ye may believe on the name of the Son of God.*

Now, it's your choice - whether or not to make this *Journey of Love*.

Chapter Two
Journey of The Word

Journeys can be fun and they can be exhausting! A lot depends on your traveling companions. And, we must all be responsible for our "part" on the journey. When I travel with my children, each persons gets their own bag and their own make-up bag and/or valise. Each person has their own set of toiletries, etc., and is responsible throughout our travels for his/her own things. This has worked out very well for us. When they were younger, the children just enjoyed having their own sets of "things", but now that they are a bit older, they have learned to become responsible for all their own toiletries and clothes when we travel, which works for us because many times we have family where we visit and one child may elect to stay with a different part of the family than another. My purpose for giving this illustration is not to inform you of how we are "SO Organized" when we travel, but to point out to you that we are ALL responsible for our own "journey" or walk with God. (Our relationship with God) We are responsible for our actions, words, every decision we make, whether they are good or evil! And, believe me, if they are not for God, they are evil!

That is not to say that whatever decisions we make that God won't be there to pick us up and love on us! It is saying, however, that sometimes we don't get all that loving up-close and personal attention from our heavenly Father as we may desire because we are not walking closer to Him! He still loves us, much like a parent who will be disappointed in a child who disobeys them, He still loves us, but the communication between us and Him is broken because we aren't walking closer to Him. I remember, as a child how wonderful I felt when hearing one of my parents praise me for doing something that pleased him or her. Just like with our earthly fathers, our heavenly Father wants to be able to praise us for obedience to Him. I know that as a child, in order to compensate for my short-comings, (which were plenty!) I probably over-compensated by pushing myself to excel in academics, etc. at school. I loved to hear my parents brag about my good grades and how well I was doing in school. That's normal - and we should desire that same praise from our heavenly Father as well. It can be like that with God if we will take the time to draw close to our Heavenly Father. How? I know that we have all probably heard this verse from God's word many times:

> *So then faith cometh by hearing and hearing*
> *By the Word of God.* ROMANS 10:17

Do you realize that by reading and meditating on God's Word, you are not only pleasing Him, but you are also building up your own faith? This is a very simple act, however, it PLEASES GOD to be communicating with you! Praise God - doesn't that phrase make you think of the song "Praise God from whom all blessings flow…."? I cannot think of those words "Praise God" without thinking of that song and wanting to add those other words "from whom all blessings flow" to it!

I used to think that reading my Bible was like a last resort. I am a reader who loves to read fiction and as a result used to find time to read the latest novels and fiction books - science fiction, medical fiction, legal fiction, it all was good as far as I was concerned. Because of that reading, however, I had little time left over to spend on reading God's Word. That has changed now. When you get into reading the Bible, you might wonder when you will have time to read anything else, because it truly is interesting! There's something for every kind of reader in the

Bible. There is some adventure, Elijah, for example. There were some really strange things happening to him throughout his life. Also, adventure in some of the stories about David and his friendship with the King's son, even though the King (Saul) was trying to kill David. There's some adventure in Joseph's life - he was imprisoned and enslaved, look at the life of Moses if you need adventure! He was raised in the home of the King, yet had to flee from it. I have been able to find romance in the book of Songs of Solomon. The book of Proverbs gives a lot of wise advice for those of us needing "self-help" books. If you will delve into the Word of God, I think you will be able to find any kind of reading you enjoy doing. The operative words being "get into the word". You will need to search out your reading material. Remember, anything that's worth anything at all requires a bit of work on your part. Personally, after reading my Bible - I can get so engrossed in it that I could lose hours at a time - I find that I get the added benefit of being so refreshed in my Spirit that I WANT to give praise to and worship God even more!

I know a lot of us have questions about our daily lives and how things in the Bible could possibly relate to them! Take it personally! I do. I used to take it personally when one of my husbands was participating in pornography and I take the Bible even more personally. God wants to be there with you every step of your life walk and He really does tell you that all throughout His Word. It's there for you in every word - you just need to get into it and search out those words that God is speaking to you. God does speak to us and communicate with us through his written word - the Bible. His word for us has not and will not change. God is the same God with the same instructions for us, the same love for us that he had for Adam and Eve. He is the same God and his Word is the same Word. His promises to you and for you have not changed, either.

If you are thinking that the Old Testament is just history and is not valid for our lives today, you are so WRONG! I'd like to remind you that Jesus came to Fulfill the law, not to eradicate it! ("Think not that I am come to destroy the law, or the prophets,

I am not come to destroy, but to fulfill." Matthew 5:17 KJV) I have been so blessed many times and find a lot of relevant information for my daily walk in the books of Isaiah and Jeremiah, the prophets! There have been many times when I felt that I just couldn't deal with things going on in my life and I would pick up my Bible and begin to read and the Psalms and Proverbs have been lifesavers for me! Truly, at times I did not know how to go on and was able to find answers in those books, sometimes through seeing what someone else did and how God led them through the same type of problem. And, the books I just referred to are all found in the Old Testament! The WHOLE book is for you! (It's for ALL of us!) Please take my advice and get into God's Word and begin to enjoy it to the exclusion of anything else - I'm not saying it's the only thing you should read, if so, you sure wouldn't be reading this, right? What I am saying is please give yourself time to find out what the Word of God can be for you! I truly believe if you will begin to read it daily, even just starting with one or two verses, that your interest will be piqued and you will want to read more and more. When we all begin to realize the importance of God's word and doing what it tells us to, applying it to our daily walks with God, that we will begin to learn how to love one another, and isn't that the Final Commandment that Jesus gave to us? To love one another as God loves us! How can we do that without an example to follow? Jesus died on the cross for us, and He was our example throughout the first four books of the New Testament. So much to read! So, what are we waiting for? So much for us to learn! So, what's our hold up? So many answers to our questions to be found in the Bible. If we really want to find the answers to our questions, we can find them in the Word of God. Do we really want the answers? If so, let's search it out in the Bible - because that's where every answer can be found for our lives today.

    If you are having difficulty finding those answers, even with a good bible containing a good Concordance in it, I would suggest a good Strong's Concordance! It's easy to use and gives you the location of where verses can be found on subject matters you may be interested in. A pastor friend once told a group I was in that if we'd read the corresponding Proverb for the number of the day, for example, if today were the first day of the month, I'd read Proverbs 1, that within several months, the wisdom there would begin to get inside our hearts and minds and that our own discernment and wisdom would begin to grow. I have been doing this for several months now, along with my other daily readings and some verses have begun to "grow" in my mind and I know in my heart, as well. This same friend suggests that you read some from the Old and New Testaments daily as well as your daily Proverb. At first, I was going to suggest that you not allow this to become a "ritual" with you because then it would be boring, but on second thought, I have to say that a GOOD ritual is not a bad thing, and really, don't understand how anything in the Bible could become so boring, except, for me, the genealogy part of it, and for those into that subject, it's not boring! And, there is a lot of reading to be enjoyed when your Bible becomes a part of you, not just words on a page!

So, taste and see that the Lord is good - eat and absorb his Word and you will find that when you begin to meditate on the things you have read, that when you need answers, they will be much easier for you to find in the Word of God. (Out of the abundance of the heart, the mouth speaks). And, you may be surprised as I have been, to find out that in circumstances when I didn't even realize I knew a specific scripture, it would come to mind. There have been times when someone needed just exactly that word from God, or times when a friend was going through certain trials and/or testings, that a verse from the Bible that I may have memorized or even just read in the past would come to mind clearly and I was able to speak it into that person's life and God has used that to his glory. Whatever is in your heart will truly come forth out of your mouth. I don't know about you, but I would very much prefer to have some sweet words from God come forth than anything else!

"Thy word have I hid in my heart that I might not sin against thee!" Psalm 119:11 Let's allow this verse to be truth in our lives - let's continue to search out the word and hide it in our hearts that when trouble comes to us (and it always does), that we may be able to stand strong in Christ because of the word that is hidden deep within our hearts that we will not sin against God.

Feel FREE to make a journey into the Word of God! Go expecting something from God - go expecting to receive something good, go expecting to have a good time, and you will not be disappointed. After all, God's Word is for YOU!

Chapter Three
Journey of Praise

Recently in the fellowship that I attend, we have had some teaching on the subject of Praise! It has been very powerful for me. Once I started to walk with Jesus on this journey, truly walk with Him, I have found how important praise is to our relationship! So, how do you praise? Well, I am going to share some forms of praise that are outlined in the Word of God and which I know you will be able to locate for yourself whenever you start to get excited about your journey and look for these in your own Bible:

Ways to Praise:

1. Lift your hands to God.
2. Clap your hands.
3. Shout unto the Lord.
4. Sing unto the Lord.
5. Dance.
6. Musical Instruments.
7. Standing.
8. Bowing down and kneeling.
9. Speaking in tongues.
10, Praise with your entire being.

These are some ways to praise that are probably pretty commonly known about in most churches or in homes where Christ has been the Center. However, these are not the only ways to praise God. When we do our daily chores required to get through life and do them as unto God, that is also praising God. Anything that we do and we dedicate it to God, that is a form of worshipping God. Our pastor has said, "When you don't know what else to do, and you've done everything you know to do, just STAND!" That in itself can be praise! Standing on the promises that God has given to you. And, every promise in God's Word is for you. Not only that, but, God has made each of us individuals with different gifts, different abilities, different dreams, and some promises that are individual to each of us according to these dreams! God is NO respecter of persons and that means that you can claim and take to heart every promise that God has made to you. Any promise in the Bible belongs to YOU!

Praise God - WHY should I praise God? Praise is very powerful - it looses things - builds faith and sends out fiery darts to the enemy's encampment. Praise is not silent or a meditation solely, although there are times when God tells us to listen. Praise is expressed - outspoken - joyfully given to God. This is where you can "let go" and be like a child in your praise time with God - you can dance and sing or enjoy whatever form of praise you chose to use to worship God with. Most of the time, our personal praise is in our own homes with just us and God present - in the privacy of our own homes, so why shouldn't we be able to let go and really praise God jubilantly! God also wants us to praise Him when we have corporate meetings (church services, meetings, etc.), and in every moment of our lives! We are to be in an attitude of worship all the time! With so many forms of worship and praise, it should never become ritual or just habit! We should all experiment with different forms of praise and be open-minded enough that whenever God tells us to change our methods of praise and/or worship, that we will do so. Don't you suppose that God enjoys some variety! Do you? I do. If you question that, just look around you at the variety in the people around you! No two people are the same, have the same number of hairs on their head, have the same thoughts exactly, no two people have exactly the same DNA, not even twins! Look at all the different colors God has used in His creation! At all the different types of flowers and even in all the different varieties of the same type of flowers, for example, roses. There are numerous types of roses! I have always heard that even no two snowflakes are alike! Wow, that's a lot of attention to detail and variety! Don't think God is going to laugh at you! He enjoys your praise and you were created to give Him praise - also, it does release you to go farther in your "journey" or walk with God. Isaiah 43:21 says: "This people have I formed for myself, they shall shew forth my praise". Wow! What does that mean to you? If you've ever wondered what your purpose on earth is, doesn't this answer that question for you? God created you and me to praise Him. We ARE "this people" that He formed for himself so that we can show forth His praise! It's that simple.

"But ye are a chosen generation, a royal priesthood, an holy nation, a peculiar people; that ye should shew forth the praises of Him who hath called you out of darkness into His marvelous light;…" this verse can be found in 1 Peter 2:9- praise Him!

Hebrews 13:15 says, "By Him therefore let us offer the sacrifice of praise to God continually, that is, the fruit of our lips giving thanks to His name." When should we give praise? Continually!!!

"Praise ye the Lord; for it is good to sing praises unto our God; for it is pleasant; and praise is comely." Do you want to be pleasing unto God? Do you want to do good? Do you want to be "comely" unto God? By the way, the word "comely" means good-looking and attractive according to Webster's Desk Dictionary. How to be attractive to God? Here's your answer! Praise ye the Lord. Do you think that God even cares what you "look like"? (On the outside?) No, the only time that is of any importance to God what you look like on the outside is whenever it becomes a problem for you - either via conceit or a concern for you!!!

I will call on the Lord, who is worthy to be praised; so shall I be saved from mine enemies. (11 Samuel 22:4) Do you need reasons to praise God? If so, here are two very good reasons!

God is worthy of your praise and He will save you from your enemies!

I will bless the Lord at all times; His praise shall continually be in my mouth. (Psalm 34:1) Wow! Another answer to the "When" question!

How to praise? Psalm 47:1, 6, 7 answers this question with "O clap your hands, all ye people; shout unto God with the voice of triumph. Sing praises to God, sing praises unto our King, sing praises. For God is the King of all the earth; sing ye praises with understanding."

Great the is the Lord and greatly to be praised in the city of our God, in the mountains of His holiness. Psalm 48:1

Whoso offered praise glorifieth me; and to him that ordereth his conversation aright will I shew the salvation of God. Psalm 50:23 - If you are to order your conversation "aright", that means that a lot of the words that enter into your normal daily conversations should be full of the Word of God - how easy to learn the Bible and be able to speak it forth if you have it in your heart, right! Praise is one easy way of getting the word into your heart because mot people seem to learn songs easier than memorizing straight data. Memorize songs that are from the Bible and you are accomplishing two things at one time! You are getting the Word into your heart - because remember that out of the heart, the mouth speaketh - and you are praising God whenever you let those words come forth! I find a lot of good ones in the book of Psalms. Here's a good example:

> *Because thy lovingkindness is better than life, my lips Shall praise thee. Thus will I bless thee (while I live): I Will lift up my hands in thy name. My soul shall be Satisfied as with marrow and fatness; and my mouth Shall praise thee with joyful lips.* Psalm 63:3-5

> *Let my mouth be filled with thy praise and with thy honor all the day. But I will hope continually, and will yet praise thee more and more.* Psalm 71:8

If we have any questions about how often to praise God or even how much, this previous verse should dispel those questions. How often: Continually. How much? More and more! We are to "hope" continually. First, you must have hope before you can develop that hope into faith! Speak the word - Sing the word, Live the word, It's a beautiful way to live. I'm not saying it's Always going to be easy - but, neither is the alternative! Journey through the Word!

It is a good thing to give thanks unto the Lord and to sing praises unto thy name, O most High. Psalm 92:1 - Who is God? "O most High" - Wow, that should be reason enough for us to praise Him! That and the fact that Jesus died for us - we should never be without that awareness in our hearts and minds.

For the Lord is great, and greatly to be praised. PSALM 96:4A

Oh that men would praise the Lord for His goodness, and for His wonderful works to the children of men! PSALM 107:8

And, at midnight Paul and Silas prayed, and sang praises unto God: and the prisoners heard them. (Acts 16:25) If you want to witness to someone, what are you going to do? Go about with an unhappy attitude all the time? Negative living is an example, alright, an example of what they DO NOT want to be!!! Praising God aloud or in the presence of those you want to testify to is in itself your testimony - Praising God allows others to see how wonderful and loving God is to you. That alone is a good testimony - let your daily life become a testimony. Allow your praises to lift up your God and He will draw others to Himself through your praises.

And be not drunk with wine, wherein is excess; but be filled with the Spirit; speaking to yourselves in psalms and hymns and spiritual songs, singing and making melody in your heart to the Lord; giving thanks always for all things unto God the Father in the name of our Lord Jesus Christ.
EPHESIANS 5:18-20

An added benefit to praising God is the "feeling" you receive! And, believe me, it feels good! This kind of feeling good has no harmful side effects! Try it and see for yourself! Some more great Bible verses for you to check out on praise are:

> PSALM 66:8 - *Praise our God, O peoples, let the sound of his praise be heard.*

> PSALM 103:1-*2 -Praise the Lord, O my soul; all my inmost being, praise his holy name. Praise the Lord, O my soul, and forget not all his benefits - who forgives all your sins and heals all your diseases, who redeems your life from the pit and crowns you with love and compassion, who satisfies your desires with good things so that your youth is renewed like the eagle's.*

WOW! I love this one! It's so powerful and impacts my whole mindset - paradigm, way of thinking, whatever you want to call it. For me, this verse goes straight to the heart and empowers me - as I pray that it does for you, too!

There's even a mention of praise and it's effect in our lives found in the midst of the prayer of faith found in James 5:13 - Is any one of you in trouble? He should pray. Is anyone happy? Let him sing songs of praise……as in a day of fasting - as one reference in the NIV Study Bible points to!

In Luke 1:46-47, there's more reference to praising God in Mary's Song - And Mary said: "My soul glorifies the Lord and my spirit rejoices in God my Savior." during her visit to Elizabeth whenever she found out that she would be the mother of Jesus. As we all know, Mary could have been fretful, anxious, ashamed of her situation, but she chose to praise God, and her heart of praise likely had a great deal to do with God's choice of her to be the earthly mother of Jesus. Praise carries weight in the kingdom of God!

Psalm 22:22-31 says: I will declare your name to my brothers; in the congregation I will praise you. You who fear the Lord, praise him! All you descendants of Jacob, honor him! Revere Him all you descendants of Israel! For he has not despised or disdained the suffering of the afflicted one, he has not hidden his face from him but has listened to his cry for help, From you comes the theme of my praise in the great assembly; before those who fear you will I fulfill my vows. The poor will eat and be satisfied; they who seek the Lord will praise him - may your hearts live forever. All the ends of the earth will remember and turn to the Lord, an all the families of the nations will bow down before him, for dominion belongs to the Lord and he rules over the nations. All the rich of the earth will feast and worship; all who go down to the dust will kneel before Him - those who cannot keep themselves alive. Posterity will serve him; future generations will be told about the Lord. They will proclaim his righteousness to a people yet unborn - for he has done it. WOW! As you know, this scripture comes just before the 23rd Psalm, which most of us could probably quote in a heartbeat! Talk about praising God - David was certainly a praiser, wasn't he! He had plenty of reasons to praise God as do each and every one of us today! What a great example for us - we can learn how to praise God by reading some of the Psalms - such as Psalm 26: 8-12 - which says: I love the house where you live, O lord, the place where your glory dwells. Do not take away my soul along with sinners, my life with bloodthirsty men, in whose hands are wicked schemes, whose right hands are full of bribes. But I lead a blameless life; redeem me and be merciful to me. My feet stand on level ground; in the great assembly I will praise the Lord. David even knew how to praise God while asking God to help him, too!

    Here's another example of praise verbalized by David in Psalm 27:4 - One thing I ask of the Lord, this is what I seek: that I may dwell in the house of the Lord all the days of my life to gaze upon the beauty of the Lord and to seek him in his temple. In the midst of another prayer asking for God's help against his enemies, David spoke these words of praise in Psalm 35:18 - I will give you thanks in the great assembly; among throngs of people I will praise you. David exhibited one form of worship we've already discussed in this chapter, that of raising your hands to God - in Psalm 28:2

where he said: "Hear my cry for mercy as I call to you for help, as I lift up my hands toward your Most Holy Place." Another praise scripture can be found in the entire chapter of Psalm 135 - it goes like this:

Praise the Lord. Praise the name of the Lord; praise him, you servants of the Lord, you who minister in the house of the Lord, in the courts of the house of our God. Praise the Lord, for the Lord is good; sing praise to his name, for that is pleasant. For the Lord has chosen Jacob to be his own, Israel to be his treasured possession. I know that the Lord is great, that our Lord is greater than all gods. The Lord does whatever pleases him, in the heavens and on the earth, in the seas and on the earth, in the seas and all their depths. He makes clouds rise from the ends of the earth; he sends lightning with the rain and brings out the wind from his storehouses. He struck down the firstborn of Egypt, the firstborn of men and animals. He sent his signs and wonders into your midst, O Egypt, against Pharaoh and all his servants. He struck down many nations and killed mighty kings - Sihon king of the Amorites, Og king of Bashan and all the kings of Canaan - and he gave their land as an inheritance, an inheritance to his people Israel. Your name, O Lord, endures forever, your renown, O lord, through all generations. For the Lord will vindicate his people and have compassion on his servants. The idols of the nations are silver and gold made by the hands of men. They have mouths but cannot speak, eyes, but they cannot see; they have ears, but cannot hear, nor is there breath in their mouths. Those who make them will be like them and so will all who trust in them. O house of Israel, praise the Lord; O house of Aaron, praise the Lord; O house of Levi, praise the Lord; you who fear him, praise the Lord. Praise be to the Lord from Zion, to him who dwells in Jerusalem. Praise the Lord. In this entire chapter, David is reminding God of how awesome and great a God he truly is. I believe that a part of our worship should be telling God how wonderful we know Him to be by reminding Him of the wonderful things that he has caused to come about in our lives. In Psalms chapter 136, the underlying theme seems to be give thanks to God for his love endures forever, it says that many times! His love endures forever! Praise Him!

In 1 Chronicles 15, verse 16 it says: David told the leaders of the Levites to appoint their brothers as singers to sing joyful songs, accompanied by musical instruments; lyres, harps and cymbals. These musicians were to sound the bronze cymbals, play the lyres, play the harps and to sing, and the priests were to blow trumpets before the ark of God. They went to bring up the ark of the covenant of God with rejoicing! They had choirs singing in rejoicing giving praise to God for the ark of the covenant. How much more now do we have to praise God for? This was not a one-time praise and worship service! This was an ongoing and regular process according to 1 Chronicles 16:4-6. And, the next several verses are a psalm of thanks from David! You know when you start listing things God has done for you and giving him the praise for them that your list grows and grows and you never seem to run out of things to praise God for! A few other verses which I won't go into at this time that mention praise are: Psalm 150:3-5 and Psalm 95:6. Like I said earlier, there are so many, these are just a sampling! I hope that these will help you get "Jump-Started" on your journey to begin to praise God and they will help you to get ideas about how to praise God as well as when and where! Remember, this is a Journey - Journey with Praise in your heart, on your lips and speak it out to God, he's just waiting to hear it from you!

One friend I know is a professional ballet dancer. Would you like to know how she sometimes expresses praise and/or worship to God? Dancing! Yes, and it is so beautiful whenever she expresses this praise in a corporate meeting. Other acquaintances I have attended church with have participated in praising God through the mediums of Mime, which, in itself is a true work of art. Another friend and I have signed to music as a form of praise and worship. Some of my family members are percussionists and practice this form of worship. So, what's holding YOU back, do you think your form of worship is just too weird or far out for God? Do you think He didn't give you that gift? So, I'd like to encourage you to feel free to worship God, using your unique talents, abilities, gifts He has given to you. One of my children is an artist and this form of praise can be seen in our home due to the use of her talents being given back to God. God has given each of us unique abilities that can be used for His glory! Remember the phrase, "Use it or lose it." Maybe your gifts have been hidden for a long time, but they can still be brought out into God's light and shared in a form of worship by giving back to God what He has given to you! God meant for your gifts to be shared in praise and worship settings to glorify and honor Him, whether it's in a private setting or in a corporate setting. That's what it's all about! It's all about HIM.

One of my favorite praise songs goes like this:

Praise Him, Praise Him, Praise Him in the morning,
Praise Him in the noontime, Praise Him, Praise Him,
Praise Him when the sun goes down.

Remember that your praise is so powerful that it can release joy on the earth as well as blessings, too! Why do you suppose that David of the Bible was a favorite of God's? PRAISE! PRAISE! PRAISE! David was a full-fledged, full-hearted worshipper! He expressed himself to God throughout the Bible and a great deal in Psalms in varying degrees and forms of worship. Even his prayers asking God to help him in stressful situations included praise. I'd like to inject here that our God is NO respecter of persons! If He honored David's praises and worship, do you think he won't honor ours?

Walking on this journey with praise is powerful, freeing and fun. I remember after a recent praise and worship session at a local church meeting I had attended with a friend, thinking that I had never had so much FUN even when I was partying out in the world and dancing the night away, and I do like to dance. It was nothing compared to the joy and peace I received during the praise and worship of this service, though! There is something missing in a lot of Christian's lives today and I believe it is the JOY that comes whenever we are able to place our faith in God and give HIM the praise and glory for everything good in our lives.

Something else about praise - a side effect or benefit, would be that I feel so much closer to God whenever I am in the midst of praising Him. And, it seems that it is so much easier for me to Hear when He speaks to me whenever I am in an attitude of praise and worship, or whenever I allow my spirit to remain in a spirit of praise throughout my daily walk with Him.

Praise God from whom all blessings flow. Walking in praise and worshipping God at every part of your journey, the good parts along with the bad, being thankful and giving God praise and thankfulness through our praise and worshipful attitudes bring blessings. It's your journey, after all, but wouldn't you rather enjoy it than to feel as if you have to struggle every mile of the way? Walk in praise and allow God's peace to rest in your being! Journey in Praise and Worship!

Chapter Four
Journey of Thankfulness

Being thankful is SO easy when everything is going your way and you are not having any kind of stress or major problem. Problems like financial stress to the point of almost losing your home on a monthly basis or like having bill collectors calling you on a daily basis, or being in abusive relationships, or dealing with rebellious children who seem to have changed overnight, or having to suddenly rely upon your 18 year old son to assist with the family's income because you just lost your job and are having problems getting one, these are all problems that I can relate to, having gone through them. However, that does not exclude me from having a heart that is thankful to God. During those times, it may be harder to be able to count your blessings, but there are always blessings to be thankful for in every situation. Not being thankful is NOT an option for Christians!

As a single mother, I had moved back to my hometown with two of my three children. The oldest was already moved back in with his father and we visited him on a regular basis. At the time we moved back to our home town, I had a full time position with a church as secretary. Four years later, that job was eliminated and I was suddenly out of a job. In the meantime, my oldest son had graduated from high school and decided he wanted to live with us. So, he moved back in with us and two months later, I was without a job. He found a good job and helped with the bills until I was able to get another full time job and take back over supporting the family. That was a major blow to my pride and was a very stressful time in my life. We managed to get through that time with the help of God and with a great deal of reduction in my pride! God knows what He's doing all the time!

At one point, both of our vehicles broke down and we had absolutely NO transportation for the four of us! On the same day, my companion, an adorable pet, was struck by a car and died, and the plumbing went beserk in our home! Well, we thought we had repaired one of the cars so I sent the children out with some friends for fun and they had to come home VERY LATE with another friend's mother because our car had caught on fire when they tried to start it! Talk about having a bad day! Whew! My first thought was not, Thank you, God for all these problems, I must confess! But, after a really good cry and asking God what to do, I did remember to thank Him for all the good in my life, that my children were safe and healthy and no harm had come to them during the course of that day, etc. Soon, that depressive cloud was lifted because by being thankful, God began to replace the depression with joy. Thankfulness will begin to bring about joy in anyone who will practice it. I remembered my verse from the Bible that says to give thanks in all things and what else can you do at that point? Pout and be upset? It sure doesn't bring about any change in your situation! Joy does! Sometimes we need to stop asking "Why me, Lord?", and start to be thankful for the good things in our lives!

Normal, carnal, earthly thinking would promote the "Why Me?" attitude and cause us to want to just give up. But, sometimes maybe we should be willing to stop and be thankful for the fact that nothing worse happened and begin to start to count our blessings. And, maybe we should be willing to check our own hearts and ask God if there is something we are supposed to be learning from this experience. I have to admit that the "Why Me?" attitude or self-pity was a reaction at first, but I refused to let it take hold or to entertain those kind of thoughts for long, because by that point in my life, I knew that God LOVED me and that He was not sending those things to happen to me to punish me for anything! It was just my day to be rained on! Have you heard that expression, "It rains on the just and the unjust"? Maybe it was just my day to get wet!

Not, it is NOT easy to be thankful in every situation. You and I can do it, though, with the help of God. We can learn to be thankful in all things on a daily basis no matter what else is happening in our lives. I'm not saying that God doesn't allow some things to happen in our lives in order to test our faith or for the edification of Himself. He will be glorified, if not by us, then by the rocks around us! Think about that, some things happen just so that God will be glorified. Some things happen to us or in our lives that are not even about us at all. They happen so that someone else can see Jesus either through the way we handled the situations or so that God will receive the glory in some manner. They might even happen just so that a seed is sown in someone else's life that will grow when properly watered by the Word at some later date and that person will be drawn to Jesus.

Whenever I am experiencing a "thankful mode", which I try to maintain for as long as possible, and as often as possible, I may be singing songs like "I bring a sacrifice of praise" and another good thanking God song is "Give thanks with a grateful heart." Being in a thankful mode is one of those times when my love of music is helpful to help me remain in a spirit of thankfulness. Music speaks to me when other methods might not at times, so, I use music to express my thankfulness to God often. I would suggest that you chose which ever method works best for you, which ever method will help you to express your thankfulness to God. Sometimes I express it through singing, writing, poetry, love letters to God, dance, just talking to God sometimes. Sometimes I like to sign for the deaf and use that method of being thankful.

Giving thanks is a beautiful expression of your love for God, too. You must know that our journey is not just earthly. It's of God and God IS love! And, He loves it whenever you express your love to Him through your thankfulness. When someone gives us a gift, it is customary to be thankful. God has given us so many gifts to be thankful for! One scripture that always encourages me to be thankful is 1 Corinthians 13. Yes, it is the "love chapter" and it is powerful - just think if we could all apply it to our lives and our dealings with one another, what an impact it could make in every phase of our lives: in politics, churches, businesses, money situations, families, everything.

I have a friend who often says "God is Good". He says it so much that sometimes people laugh and know almost when he's going to say it. But, you see, he is so very thankful to be living in the United States. He is from another country where there is much poverty and very few freedoms. He knows the difference in the countries from past experiences and so appreciates the opportunity to live in a "rich" country! This friend has seen so many horrible things in his country that he is so thankful for every day and every benefit he receives living in the United States. He is so thankful for every day that he has contact with spirit-filled Christians who are trying to walk out this journey of love. If you were around this friend for very long, you would notice that any spirits of depression or oppression seem to lift when you are in his presence - because of his thankfulness!

We have SO much to be thankful for! I know you are probably tired of hearing that expression, but please consider it - it is the TRUTH. I am so thankful for Christian parents and the childhood that they gave to me, what a precious gift. And, I am very thankful that they are still around and living in the same city as me. My three children are also gifts that I am continually thankful for. Have you considered that we have our lives to be thankful for, our country, our freedom, both in the religious realms and freedom of speech. I know that there is always controversy about something in the religious realms that Satan is constantly trying to see that some of our religious beliefs are not as free as they have been, yet we still have a lot more religious freedom than many countries where we could have been placed! We sometimes need to remind ourselves to be thankful for the shelter and vehicles and family and friends that God has placed in our lives, too.

Do not for a minute think that you cannot find SOMETHING in your life, no matter how small it may seem, to be thankful for!

Every one of us has a LIST of things to be thankful for. Make a list, count your blessings and just be thankful for every last one of those items on your thanksgiving list! Thanksgiving should be every day for those of us who are Christians! If we are saved and walking with God, we have everything to be thankful for. If you cannot think of one thing to be thankful for, be thankful that God loves you and that He has promised you in Isaiah that "…no weapon formed against you shall prosper…". (If you are his child, you have that promise!) Wow! Just knowing that because I am a child of God, that when Satan comes against me and wants to form his weapons of despair, depression, harm to me, that his weapons cannot prosper because I have God's promise that no weapon formed against me will be able to prosper! I know that once I start making a thanksgiving list, I can never seem to complete it!

We can all be thankful that God gave His only Son to die on the Cross for us and that Jesus arose again, fulfilling the prophecies of the Old Testament. My oldest son is now 19 and just thinking about him leaving home any time soon - well, it's not a good thought for this particular Mom anyway. And, I cannot imagine having to give him up for someone who does not love him and does not want his best and who does not want to walk with him! Do you get the picture? Imagine the difficulty of giving up one of your own children and then think of all the horrible things that Jesus WILLINGLY went through so that YOU and I could be reconciled to a God who loves us so much that He gave His only son to die for us! Do you realize that if YOU were the only person on this earth who was in need of reconciliation with God, that He would have sent Jesus to die on the cross JUST FOR YOU!

Give Thanks - it will make your journey so much more pleasant, too! People enjoy being around people with good attitudes! You will notice that you become a much more pleasant person to be around whenever you have a thankful spirit and are of a more positive attitude all the time!

Colossians 3:15 says: "And let the peace of God rule in your hearts, to the which also ye are called in one body, and be ye thankful."

Philippians 4:6, 7 says: "Be careful for nothing; but in every thing by prayer and supplication with thanksgiving let your request be made known unto God. And the peace of God, which passeth all understanding, shall keep your hearts and minds through Christ Jesus." If we will be thankful letting our requests be known to God, we reap the bonus of having our hearts and minds kept through Jesus Christ! Let's joyfully walk on this journey of thankfulness!

Chapter Five
Journey of Forgiveness

Do you know the meaning of "forgive"? Well, my dictionary indicates that to forgive is to pardon, to give up resentment of, to cease resentment against! To me that means we are to take action - not just word service! We must make a conscious decision to "forgive". You have probably always heard the expression "… forgive and forget…", well, maybe we should look at it the way our Heavenly Father does!!! At one point in my life, a friend was praying for me regarding a matter that I had shared with her and God gave her this word for me: "It's as though it never happened!" That is exactly the way God looks at sins we have committed and repented of - He forgives us when we ask Him and immediately forgets them. Have you heard that song, "What sins are you talking about?" How appropriate! Sometimes we want to remind Him of our sins and sometimes we may have a harder time forgiving ourselves and may have a tendency to bring them up again and again in our conversations with our Father, who doesn't even remember what we are talking about, because, He's ALREADY FORGOTTEN THEM! So, we are, in reality, wasting our time and His by reminding Him of those things that he has NO memory of!

Forgiveness can be so much simpler than we actually think! So many times we want to make it harder, maybe because we are not really willing or ready to forgive someone - after all, who doesn't enjoy nursing an old hurt at one time or another, right?

Whoops! May have hit a soft spot on that one! That's alright, we all have them, and I do deal with issues in forgiveness as well as anyone else.

Nobody wants to admit that it is our own willfulness that keeps us from forgiving someone for what we consider needs forgiving! In the first place, maybe we should consider if that "thing" we're holding onto like a child holding a balloon in the air (letting it float around with little or no restriction - and floating through our minds just when we think we have it all together!) - if that is really worth holding onto!! Whoa! Which one of us can honestly say that right now we aren't remembering something that we consider needs to be forgiven -- whether it's something we have said or done to someone else or a hurt that we are harboring within ourselves that we need to release forgiveness to someone else for?

I was told one time that if we sincerely speak forgiveness to someone - even though within ourselves we may not have the strength or ability to forgive (pardon - to release from liability of an offense!) that person at that time without divine assistance, that speaking it to them would allow you the freedom to open your heart and allow God to BEGIN that work within you and before long, without even realizing it sometimes - because sometimes God's work is so subtle that you may or may not notice it happening, then you may realize some time later - maybe hours, days, weeks or months later that you truly do love that person and have forgiven them.

Have you heard of that song, "Our God is an Awesome God"? doesn't that just apply here - Our God is an awesome God, He reigns in Heaven above, with wisdom, grace and love, our God is an awesome God. When we need to forgive someone else, those qualities are needed, wisdom, grace and love.

Our God is an awesome God who truly loves each and every one of us and wants us to be able to fulfill our destiny within His perfect will - however, walking in forgiveness is truly necessary in order for us to be able to begin our walk in Him. The simple act of forgiveness should be simple for all of us, although, I confess there were times that I wanted to continue to blame my ex-husbands for the things that went wrong in our marriages. It was so much easier for me because if I could continue to blame everything on them, then I did not have to forgive them! Ha Ha. That's what I thought!

How wrong I was. Even though a number of their actions were wrong and some did include abuse, I still had to forgive them, not even for themselves, but so that I could grow in my walk with God. It was necessary for me to lay down those bitter feelings and bad memories and give them to God first and ask God to forgive me, then it was necessary for me to forgive them.

Let me tell you a funny one - when I was a small girl, probably about 7 or 8 years of age, one time my mother told me that my ears stuck out funny like Mickey Mouse's ears! For many years, I held that hurt within me and was very self conscious about my ears. I held that hurt way into adulthood and for a long time wouldn't even let my ears show through my hair, making sure nobody was able to see them. Well, if you knew me, you'd know that is certainly not the most prominent feature on my face and probably never was! For many years, I harbored that painful phrase "ears like Mickey Mouse's" and guess what! My mother didn't even remember saying that to me! When I asked her one time about it, she didn't remember saying it. Boy, did I feel stupid! And, talk about unforgiveness, that's a long time to carry something around that nobody even remembers! And, in reality, most people wouldn't even remember saying something so minor! That's one reason why I said earlier on that we really need to consider why we are holding onto those hurts sometimes, is it really worth hurting all that time when maybe that person really didn't even know he or she was hurting you and had NO intention of hurting you? Just as my mother meant absolutely nothing by a frivolous remark, probably spoken in jest and I really took it to heart for years and then had to go through the entire forgiveness process over something so trivial!

Maybe we are hurting unnecessarily! Maybe we need to not be so sensitive! (Ouch! I know that one was painful for me, too! Please try to see where I am coming from here, though.) Many times we take on hurts that are unnecessary because we are too sensitive and therefore we create an atmosphere of sensitivity to become hurt too easily. I KNOW that there are people who have sincerely hurt us, sometimes intending to do so. Some of them don't realize what they're doing, also. One of my ex-husbands was deeply involved in various forms of pornography and he is currently paying the consequences. He was also very abusive and controlling throughout the short marriage. He is now living in a prison cell, with a life sentence. This one required a LOT of forgiveness, some of which I am continuing to walk through. But, God is SO good, and so loving, and so forgiving that if I am going to walk on this journey of love with my Heavenly Father, how can I NOT forgive him? No, I am not saying it has been easy because some things happened during that 3 year period that required some Christian counseling for me and my children - yet, God forgives, and even though this man has never confessed to me all that he did and has never asked for my forgiveness, it is still necessary that I forgive him. In order for me to move forward in my walk with God, I knew that I would have to go through the forgiveness process with this man. And I believe that I am well on the way to total forgiveness with him. Do you know how? Every day I pray for him and ask God to forgive me for harboring resentment and unforgiveness in my heart. Any time he comes to mind, I pray this prayer. Recently, I realized that whenever this person's name was brought up by someone in the course of a conversation that the strong hatred that I felt for him was not there and that God was releasing me from him through forgiveness. It took me asking God to forgive me first, though. And, I know that God has forgiven me and is allowing me to pass that forgiveness on to someone to whom I needed to forgive. If God did it for me and He is no respecter of persons, He will do the same for you. Remember, that if you were the only person on this earth who needed to have it proven to you just how much God loves you, that God would have sent Jesus to die on the cross just for you! That's how much he loves you. That's how much he loves me. When Jesus was dying on the cross, FOR US, and God literally had to turn

His back on the scene because He could not stand to see His Son die. Remember, He is THE FATHER, and He loves His Son, too! However, He allowed it to continue because He loves us that much. And, even though it was for OUR sins that Jesus died, God is still willing to forgive us with open arms and to welcome us Home to Him if we will just ask!

If we "earthly" or "carnal" human beings cannot grasp that with our minds, once our hearts have been washed with the blood of Jesus - reconciled with God, then it is easier to understand, especially if we have been building our faith in God by reading and absorbing His Word! So many times God forgave the people in the Bible because He loved them so much.

Let's look at a good example - King David! While David was a King, he was involved in murder and adultery. Yet, he was the "apple of God's eye"! Was something wrong with God's eyesight? NO. David had a heart for God and repented and just because God loved him so much, He forgave him when David asked Him to. Is God any more fond of David than He is of you? NO! What does that mean? God is ready and willing to forgive us, too.

There's no more refreshing feeling than cleanliness. Do you want to feel spiritually clean? There is no more refreshing bath than when you allow God's forgiveness to wash over you and you will NEVER feel more clean in your entire life, I can promise you that! How hard is it? Well, whenever I used to attend a certain un-named church, they used to teach a simple ABC trick, it was:

A   Ask
B   Believe
C   Confess

I would like to add a few more to that, even though they don't fall in alphabetical order! The first one is to RECEIVE. When you accept the fact that Jesus died for you and ask Him to come into your heart and reign over your life and you believe that Jesus died and rose again and you confess it with your mouth and receive all that God has for you, wow! Then, I'd like to suggest that you allow yourself to soak in it! Soak in that wonderful feeling for a while. One of my favorite parts of my schedule is when I take the time to "soak in a tub of bubbles" for as long as possible. That is the same picture I want you to get, one of soaking in God's goodness, allowing yourself to soak it all in, because you will need it very soon afterwards and the more you absorb into yourself, the more strength you will have to fight Satan. So, allow that wonderful feeling of God's forgiveness to wash all over you, soak in God's love as a result of you receiving His forgiveness. Even though we do not live by feelings alone, we are given these feelings to help us support our faith. I'd much rather feel good in a good soak, than not, wouldn't you? Soak in God's love, read your Bible, there's so much for you there. Many verses are dedicated to forgiveness, here are just a few I'd like to share with you:

Psalm 25:16-18 - "Turn thee unto me and have mercy upon me; for I am desolate and afflicted. The troubles of my heart are enlarged, O bring thou me out of my distress. Look upon mine affliction and my pain; and forgive all my sins." This was David crying out to God. Don't ever think that you have done something SO bad that God cannot forgive you. Hello! Look at David's history - read ALL the Psalms to start with! You'll find that David was not a perfect man. However, he was FORGIVEN more than once!! If you are having some problems that require that you are forgiven more than once, don't give up and think that God is tired of forgiving you for the same thing over and over again or even different things, just so much sin, or whatever, God is BIGGER than any sin you may have committed! God is no respecter of persons! If he did it for David, He will do it for you! Don't you believe that God will forgive you as many times as Jesus told Peter to forgive? (70 times 7 for each and every offense?) Not in one day, for each and every offense!!! You must be convinced by now that God really loves YOU, he knows your name, your address, your lifestyle, your likes and dislikes, your everything! Face it friend, HE KNOWS YOU and He loves you anyway! He is waiting for you to come home to Him. He is so willing to forgive you, so, WALK IN FORGIVENESS, let God love you and soak in it!

Psalm 25:11 says "For thy name's sake, O Lord, pardon mine iniquity; for it is great." It doesn't matter how "great" your sin is or how much you have done that is wrong or sinful - God loves YOU - He is waiting for you to ask for His forgiveness so that he can shower you with His love.

If it seems that I am repetitive in this Chapter, it is only because I want you to get it! I know that television commercials use repetition - they will say the same thing over and over and over again until you get it "stuck" in your head and your brain just can't seem to get rid of the little jingles - well, that's the idea here! Here's a jingle I'd like to get stuck in all of our heads: GOD LOVES ME, GOD LOVES ME, GOD LOVES ME!!! GOD IS NO RESPECTER OF PERSONS!! GOD IS NO RESPECTER OF PERSONS!! GOD IS NO RESPECTER OF PERSONS!!

Nothing anyone can say to you would be more important than those things that you share with your Heavenly Father. Some of my most precious times are those that I spend with my Father, let me tell you, a lot of things have been thrown at me by Satan, and some things I have allowed to happen in my life through the consequences of my bad decisions or wrong choices, however, these days, I don't question if God truly loves me! I know He does. I finally "got" it inside of me and it has taken way too long! I'd hate to see anyone else go this long without the realization of how much God loves them!

I want you to be able to get in on that wonderful love, forgiveness, cleanness, that purity of heart that you have whenever you are walking with God. Let me tell you that nobody on this earth can do that for you!!! I should know, been there, done that, (as the teens say), married four times, thinking that this time, this husband would be able to fulfill my needs. No way, I was looking in the wrong places! God is the only one who can complete you and fulfill all your needs. I am just like everybody else when it comes to "wants". I want a nice home, furniture, car, the best haircut, jewelry, all that "stuff" like most people. But, the most important thing I want NOW is God. I want God to come before the stuff in my life. (Seek ye first the kingdom of God and all these other things will be given to you. Matthew 6:33) God is the only one who can and will totally satisfy all your needs. We just need to stop looking to other things for satisfaction and look to God.

God has renewed my life in so many ways. I will share this very personal history with you - understand it is personal to me, and you may or may not relate to it. As I indicated at the beginning of this book, I was raised in a family of four. One sister, my mother and Dad and me. We were as normal a household as they come, I guess, who can be the judge of that? Anyway, I grew up always feeling inferior to my younger sister, who was an outstanding athlete. She had a lot of athletic abilities that I did not possess and I was not the least bit athletically inclined. As a result of my comparing myself to her in that area and coming up short, I was very competitive with her and used my own academic skills to compete with her. I felt that in order to gain my parent's favor or attention, it was necessary for me to compete with my sister. (Keep in mind, this was my mindset, and not necessarily that of my parents!) And, I always felt that because my father had no boys and circumstances brought different things into my life and my sister's, that my father favored my sister over me, because of her athletic abilities. Do you know how old I was before I was able to confess this to God and ask forgiveness and to release forgiveness to my father? Would you believe 40+ years of age! I don't want anyone else to go that long with those kind of feelings, that is the reason I am sharing this bit of history with you! Was it worth holding onto? NO! Nothing is. Release forgiveness and move on! If you aren't able to release forgiveness within yourself for whatever reasons, and most of us can't, God is there to help you and He will if you will ask Him to. Isn't it nice to know that you don't have to walk alone? Believe me, forgiveness can be very freeing, both whenever you release it to someone else or if you are on the receiving end! Just a side note, also, if that person doesn't even know that you need to forgive them, make it a private release! Don't publicize it. If they don't even know that you feel the need to forgive them for something, it only causes confusion if you go to them and announce to them that you are forgiving them for stepping on your toes twenty years ago for something they are not going to remember doing or saying or however that hurt came about! But, if they are aware of the problem, it will bring about healing for both of the parties involved to forgive them and let them know they are forgiven.

The Bible says … "For if ye forgive men their trespasses, your heavenly Father will also forgive you; but if ye forgive not men their trespasses, neither will your Father forgive your trespasses." (Matthew 6:14, 15) I don't know about you, but I would very much like to be forgiven for ALL my trespasses, so, I am going to forgive those who have trespassed against me - whether it was a "major" matter or something trivial like the "Mickey Mouse" ears!

Matthew 18:21, 22 says: "Then came Peter to him (Jesus) and said, Lord how oft shall my brother sin against me and I forgive him? Till seven times? Jesus saith unto him, I say not unto thee, Until seven times, but, until seventy times seven.

"Take heed to yourselves; if thy brother trespass against thee, rebuke him; and if he repent, forgive him." Luke 17:3 - To me this tells us that when we are feeling offended by someone or if someone has "trespassed" against us (done something to us that would require forgiveness), then we are to:

#1 *Go to that person and tell them what we feel they have done to offend us*

Or "rebuke" them and

#2 *Give them the opportunity to repent (say they're sorry)*

and

#3 *Forgive them!*

"And when ye stand praying, forgive, if ye have aught against any; that your Father also which is in heaven may forgive you your trespasses." MARK 11:25

"Forbearing one another, and forgiving one another, if any man have a quarrel against any, even as Christ forgave you, so also do ye." COLOSSIANS 3:13

Again, in the foregoing two verses, it is apparent that we are not to "hold in" those things that "hurt" us or require for us to forgive someone else, but to confront the issue and thereby get it over and done with!

"Brethren, I count not myself to have apprehended; but this one thing I do, forgetting those things which are behind, and reaching forth unto those things which are before. I press toward the mark for the prize of the high calling of God in Christ Jesus." Philippians 3:13, 14 This verse tells us to then forget it, right? "…forgetting those things which are behind…" that means the PAST!! Forget the past and get on with your forward walk with God. We are walking forward, not backward, right? "Remember ye not the former things, neither consider the things of old, behold I will do a new thing, now it shall spring forth; shall ye not know it? I will even make a way in the wilderness, and rivers in the desert." (Isaiah 43:18, 19) "Remember ye not the former things…" - to me that indicates that we cannot hold onto the old hurts of the past - former things- and "neither consider the things of old". I don't know about you, but I don't want to miss out on the "…new things" referred to in the same verse when God says "Behold I will do a new thing; now it shall spring forth; shall ye not know it?" I don't want to have my plate so full of bitterness, hate, resentment, unforgiveness, etc., that there's no room for me to be able to experience the "new thing" that God is doing.

"For this is thankworthy, if a man for conscience toward God endure grief, suffering wrongfully, for what glory is it, if, when ye be buffeted for your faults, ye shall take it patiently? but if, when ye do well, and suffer for it, yet take it patiently, this is acceptable with God. For even hereunto were ye called, because Christ also suffered for us, leaving us an example, that ye should follow his steps; who did not sin, neither was guile found in his mouth, who, when he was reviled, reviled not again; when he suffered, he threatened not; but committed himself to Him that judgeth righteously. These were words written about Jesus by Peter in 1 Peter 2:19-23. If we need an example for our lives, there it is. Jesus did it, so can we! Maybe you're thinking, "Right, Jesus was the Son of God, so, of course, HE could do it!" But, we're just human beings - Please remember you are not alone in this! God gave us the Holy Spirit to help us. We also have the ability to stay filled with the Holy Spirit, which is the reason that when Jesus became a "son of man", He was able to do all that He did - He also had the Holy Spirit . Again, remember that God is no respecter of persons! We have been adopted into God's family through salvation - through the blood of Jesus Christ whenever we have accepted Jesus into our hearts and confessed our sins before God - we have the ability to carry the Holy Spirit within us at all times. I would like to challenge each one reading this book today to try it! If Jesus was able to forgive those men who were in the process of killing him, yet, Jesus took a moment to pray for the Father's forgiveness on them, then, I don't see how we can think of doing anything other than forgiving one another! I'll reinforce something stated earlier, maybe we are not at a place yet where we can do it without a great deal of prayer and without God's help. But GOD CAN. (refer to Luke 23:34)

Do you think you can stand a little bit more about forgiveness? How about this verse: "Blessed are they which are persecuted for righteousness' sake; for theirs is the kingdom of Heaven. Blessed are ye, when men shall revile you and persecute you, and shall say all manner of evil against you falsely, for my sake. Rejoice, and be exceedingly glad; for great is your reward in heaven; for so persecuted they the prophets which were before you." If we want rewards in heaven, we can surely handle a little persecution, right? Forgiveness is where it starts. "For we know him that hath said,

Vengeance belongeth unto me, I will recompense, saith the Lord. And again, The Lord shall judge His people." Hebrews 10:30

If we are holding onto old hurts and resentments built up over the years, then we are really putting ourselves in God's place by judging other people's actions, deeds, motives, etc., and we are trying, in a very subtle way to handle the vengeance on our own. Pretty strong statement, but if we would really consider our own motives, we might find it to be true!

Here is another Bible verse that is very applicable to this subject: "Beloved, think it not strange concerning the fiery trial which is to try you, as though some strange thing happened unto you; But rejoice, inasmuch as ye are partakers of Christ's sufferings; that, when his glory shall be revealed, ye may be glad also with exceeding joy. If ye be reproached for the name of Christ, happy are ye; for the spirit of glory and of God resteth upon you; on their part he is evil spoken of, but on your part he is glorified." 1 Peter 4:12-14

> *"But, I say unto you, Love your enemies, bless them that curse you, do good to them that hate you, and pray for them which despitefully use you, and persecute you."* MATTHEW 5:44

"Be not overcome of evil, but overcome evil with good." Romans 12:21 How are you or I going to be able to overcome evil with good and not be overcome by it without walking in forgiveness?

> *"Not rendering evil for evil, or railing for railing; but contrariwise blessing; knowing that ye are thereunto called, that ye should inherit a blessing. For he that will love life, and see good days, let him refrain his tongue from evil, and his lips that they speak no guile."* 1 PETER 3:9, 10

I guess that means that when somebody does wrong to us, we are not justified in going about town telling everyone about it!!! OUCH!!! We are required by God to forgive them and Bless them, too! Wow, that requires a lot from us, doesn't it! Yes, it does. Will it be worth it? Yes, it will be worth everything.

Another verse I'd like to discuss with you is Ephesians 4:31, 32, which states: "Let all bitterness and wrath and anger, and clamour, and evil speaking, be put away from you, with all malice. And be ye kind one to another, tender-hearted, forgiving one another, even as God for Christ's sake hath forgiven you." Even when we know we are right, when we know we are justified in feeling hurt, we still have to forgive, God has commanded us to forgive and put away all malice, just like God forgave us.

Some additional verses on forgiveness that you might like to research for yourself are:

Ephesians 1:6,7	Psalm 85:2
Jeremiah 33:8	II Corinthians 5:17
Psalm 103:12	I John 2:1
I John 1:9	Hebrews 8:12
Isaiah 55:7	Colossians 2:13
Mark 11:25	Isaiah 1:18
Psalm 32:1-2	Isaiah 43:25

I'd like to challenge you to step out on faith and forgive. If you do not feel capable of doing this on your own, ASK GOD to help you. Speak out the forgiveness, if they don't know about it, speak it out between you and God. If the other person knows about the situation, go to them, in a non-confrontational way and love on them and release forgiveness to them. Forgive and forget -- after all, you want your sins and trespasses against others to be forgiven, right? Walk in forgiveness along your journey of love.

Chapter Six
Journey of Faith

> *"Faith is the substance of things hoped for, the evidence of things not seen."* Hebrews 11:1

Faith moves mountains - see for yourself in Matthew 17:20, 21 - it says: "And Jesus said unto them, Because of your unbelief, for verily I say unto you, If ye have faith as a grain of mustard seed, ye shall say unto this mountain, Remove hence to yonder place and it shall remove; and nothing shall be impossible unto you." He also went on to say in the following verse: "Howbeit this kind goeth not out but by prayer and fasting." I know we would much rather leave this part out sometimes, but, we really cannot discount it, especially as it was all one response at one time from Jesus to the disciples when asked why they were unable to cast out demons from a man's son who was considered at that time to be a "lunatic".

Faith is the opposite of unbelief. To have faith, you must BELIEVE!!! Believe in Jesus, God the Father, and the Holy Spirit, your comforter! There's a song we used to sing a long time ago - some of the song is like this: "I believe in Jesus, I believe in God..." Simply believing is the beginning of your faith. In order to build on that faith, we must read the word, study and meditate on the word. What is the word? God's word is the Bible. Some people call it the "Good Book". Whichever name you chose, it is God's word to you and for you and you will find life and sustenance there. You will be able to draw strength for your daily walk on this journey with God - and if you will continue to peruse your "word", you will find many answers to questions about your daily walk with Christ, as well as many helpful verses to aide you in your praise and worship time. You will find instruction for your life there, although it may be necessary for you to study, pray and meditate on the word in order to get what you need from it. Don't expect to just be able to open up the Bible every time you open it up and randomly find the answers you are searching for! It may be necessary to invest some time and effort into your search. That's not to say that sometimes when you are in dire need of answers and that you can't ask God to lead you to a scripture to help you, because you can do that and He will guide you in that way. I have experienced that before and heard many testimonies of others doing the same thing. My point here, however, is that you will - most of the time- need to spend some time perusing the Word to find answers to assist you in your walk with Christ. If you will be willing to spend some time in the Word, you will be richly blessed as a result of your time invested. It will build up your faith!

> *"So, then faith cometh by hearing, and hearing by the word of God."* ROMANS 10:17

> *"For I say, through the grace given unto me, to every man that is among you, not to think of himself more highly than he ought to think; but to think soberly, according as God hath dealt to every man the measure of faith."* ROMANS 12:3

> *"For we walk by faith, not by sight."* II CORINTHIANS 5:7

Walking by faith and not by sight to me has been a difficult, but rewarding leg of the journey. It has meant for me, that I have had to trust God to be my financial provider at times when I have always been used to being the "breadwinner" in my home. I was always the "responsible" half of the marriage, the one who was responsible for the wellbeing of my three children and myself in between marriages and even during most of the marriages. Even though I had been married a part of the time, it was still necessary that I work in order to provide the necessities for the family. So, walking by faith meant for me that when I was OUT of work, it was necessary for me to totally trust God for provision and I had to place my trust in God and allow Him to provide instead of me trying to always be in control. I had to become totally dependent upon Him. God has been a wonderful provider for us - He has not allowed us to go without any good thing that we needed. (Just as He has promised in His word!) We never had a utility cut off, we always had plenty of food and clothing and shelter! He always provided!

I am continuing to walk through a part of the journey where God is continuing to teach me about His companionship and love. There have been times in the recent past that I have cried out to God that I needed someone to talk to for some direction in my life and He is always there and gives me that instruction, direction, or faith-builders through His word. You can always find what you need in His word, at least that has been my experience. And, as I have stated earlier in this book, the way we build our faith is through His word. It has been such a blessing to me to be able to open up my Bible and read and find answers. And, usually they are so simple and can be applied to our daily lives so simply!

Hebrews 12:2 says "Looking unto Jesus the author and finisher of our faith, who for the joy that was set before him endured the cross, despising the shame, and is set down at the right hand of the throne of God." Jesus is the author and Jesus is the finisher of our faith. He wrote the story! (author) And, he's with us until the end (finisher)! Once we have accepted Jesus into our hearts and begin our walk on this journey of love with Him, he is there to the end - he will finish our faith. "For therein is the righteousness of God revealed from faith to faith; as it is written, the just shall live by faith." (Romans 1:17) "Just" here refers to us - you and me- because once we have accepted Jesus into our hearts, at that point we start to become the righteousness of God in Christ and we become "just". We are justified through the blood of Jesus! Living from faith to faith sometimes can be a rollercoaster ride, but it can be exciting and fun at the same time! I want to emphasize that if we are grounded in the word of God - thereby building our faith, we will not have as many dramatic highs and lows, it will become a smoother ride if we can just continue to walk in faith - irregardless of what is happening in our lives.

"But without faith, it is impossible to please him, for he that cometh to God must believe that He is, and that He is a rewarder of them that diligently seek Him." Hebrews 11:6 There's another good reason to continue on in faith - to be able to please God!

> "Whom having not seen, ye love; in whom, though now ye see Him not, yet believing, ye rejoice with joy unspeakable and full of glory; receiving the end of your faith, even the salvation of your souls." 1 PETER 1:7-9

Formerly, I stated that Jesus was the finisher of our faith as indicated in Hebrews 12:2 - Now, look at that in relation to 1 Peter 1:9 "Receiving the end of your faith, even the salvation of your souls." As the finisher of our faith, Jesus is also the savior of our souls.

"For whatsoever is born of God overcometh the world; and this is the victory that overcometh the world, even our faith. 1 John 5:4 We will become overcomers of the world through our faith!!! I don't know about you, but to me that is very exciting!

"And, behold a woman, which was diseased with an issue of blood 12 years came behind him, and touched the hem of his garment, for she said within herself, if I may but touch his garment, I shall be whole. But, Jesus turned him about, and when he saw her, he said, Daughter, be of good comfort; thy faith hath made thee whole." Matthew 9:20-22. If God is no respecter of persons and I believe that to be true, then if her faith resulted in her total healing of a 12 year old malady, God can and will do it for you or me as a result of us practicing our faith! Notice, I said "practicing" because sometimes it requires some action on our parts - just as the woman had to reach out and touch His garment in order to receive her healing, through her faith. She practiced her faith by reaching out to Jesus!

"Is any sick among you? Let him call the elders of the church; and let them pray over him anointing him with oil in the name of the Lord; and the prayer of faith shall save the sick, and the Lord shall raise him up." James 5:14, 15a What does this verse speak to you? Again, since God is no respecter of persons, if He did it for them in the days of the Bible and the entire Bible is for us today, then we have to understand that God will do it for us today, also, if we will just practice our faith.

"Jesus said unto him, If thou canst believe, all things are possible to him that believeth." Mark 9:23 If you can believe, all things are possible to you, Rhonda. If you can believe, all things are possible to you, John, Mary, Belinda, whatever your name is, put your name in there and see how it affects your thinking! If I can just believe, anything is possible in my life! There's a song we used to sing in one church I used to attend growing up, it was called "Nothing is Impossible", some of the words are "…Nothing is impossible when you put your trust in God, Nothing is Impossible when you put your faith in Him…" How true!

My advice to anyone at this time is to earnestly and diligently seek God, because as Hebrews 11:6 says, "But without faith it is impossible to please Him; for he that cometh to God must believe that He is, and that He is a rewarder of them that diligently seek Him." It only requires a small amount of faith to begin your journey of faith with God and let it grow from there!

Chapter Seven
Journey of Obedience

To be obedient means to be submissive. The word "obey" means to comply with orders. One of the verses I have had to remind myself of many times is this one: "Behold, to obey is better than sacrifice, and to hearken than the fat of the rams." This verse is found in 1 Samuel 15:22b. For a period of time in my life, after being a "working mom" for the entire time I have had children (19 years now), I have found myself in a position where I have not been able to return to full time employment yet. I had received prophetic words from many leaders that I was to stay home with my children for a period of time. It turns out this period of time has been approximately eight months. And, it turns out this was a very important time during the younger ones' lives. Me being off during this time was beneficial for both of the younger children. I heeded God's words to me and obeyed what I believed that God was telling me to do. It was necessary for me to obey God and not worry about 'Man's" opinions. Believe me, several key people in my life did not agree with me staying home with the children during this time period, however, it is more important to me to obey God than to worry about someone else's opinion of me! God was faithful to supply every need and honored my obedience to Him. It was not EASY for me to do this, I have worked most of my life and yet it was a very rewarding time!

I had people telling me that because my older son was working and helping with the bills during this time that I was an "infidel" because I was not the one providing for the majority of financial support for me and my children. Keep in mind, I am a woman, and, consider myself to be a woman of God. God has made many differences in the roles of women and men and their responsibilities throughout the Bible. I was "torn" between being the provider and spending more time just being "Mom"! After approximately eight months of living like this, being totally dependent upon God's provision for us, and being obedient to His will for me and my children, during my prayer time, when I was speaking to God about this situation, He gave me a release to return back to full time employment. Now, I realize the importance of LISTENING to God and then OBEYING God when He speaks to us, irregardless of what everyone else around us is saying, listen to GOD! You will have to be in tune with God through your prayer life and have faith in order to be able to obey His instructions for you. And, I know He speaks different words of instruction to each of us, however, they can all be verified in the Bible. If you aren't able to find them in the Bible, you may not be hearing God!

During that time of unemployment, I was able to become more involved in ministry and donated some of my time and skills to assist my pastor as his unpaid secretary for several months. God was so faithful to us during that time that we never once went without food - didn't even come close, and we never had a utility cut off and we were well dressed. God did not forget about taking care of us in any way. He is faithful to complete in you that which He has begun!

Proverbs 25:12 says: "As an earring of gold (valuable) and an ornament of fine gold, so is a wise reprover upon an obedient ear."

Obedience is so important to your walk throughout this journey of love. Which means that we have to battle with the different forms of rebellion that seem to crop up in our lives because if we are walking in rebellion of any type, it is very difficult to be obedient to the word of God. In fact, I would venture to say that an act of obedience is in direct opposition to an act of rebellion!

Isaiah 1:19 says: "If ye be willing and obedient, ye shall eat the good of the land." Now, I am not a prosperity preacher, however I do see the wisdom in being obedient so that we can prosper, don't you? Especially after having it spelled out to us by Isaiah in the aforementioned verse.

In Matthew, Chapter 8, where Jesus was resting in the boat crossing the waters when a storm arose and he "rebuked the winds and the sea, and there was a great calm" (found in Matthew 8:26b), and in verse 27, where it says "But the men marveled, saying What manner of man is this, that even the winds and the sea obey him!" We should be just as in awe of Jesus and be willing to obey Him. We should be willing to obey our Heavenly Father when he gives us instructions. Obey without a shred of rebellion or questioning God. Sometimes I think we question God because we know NOT to rebel, but we have rebellion in our hearts and that question is simply a delay tactic! God controls everything in our lives, God is in control, God KNOWS what He's doing! He tells the winds and the seas what to do and they OBEY Him! If that is not an awesome God, then, I don't know what is! If the "nature" in life can be controlled by a simple rebuke from Jesus, then we have to see that God is in control of everything and stop worrying and just rest in His love by being obedient to Him.

If you have difficulty understanding how to be strong and obey God when all around you are saying do something else or you really would prefer to have your own way (rebellion), you might try some of the following verses on strength that I have researched for use in my own life:

> DANIEL 10:19 - "O man greatly beloved, fear not; peace be unto thee, be strong, yea, be strong. And when he had spoken unto me, I was strengthened, and said, Let my Lord speak; for thou hast strengthened me."

> "My soul melteth for heaviness; strengthen thou me according unto thy word. (David crying out to God) PSALM 1198:28

> ISAIAH 30:15 - *"For thus saith the Lord God, the Holy One of Israel; In returning and rest shall ye be saved; in quietness and in confidence shall be your strength."*

(You've always heard of the strong, silent type, where do you think that came from? Ha Ha!)

"That He would grant you, according to the riches of His glory, to be strengthened with might by His Spirit in the inner man; that Christ may dwell in your hearts by faith; that ye, being rooted and grounded in love." EPHESIANS 3:16, 17

> COLOSSIANS 1:10-12 - *"That ye might walk worthy of the Lord unto all pleasing, being fruitful in every good work, and increasing in the knowledge of God. Strengthened with all might, according to His glorious power, unto all patience and longsuffering with joyfulness; giving thanks unto the Father which hath made us meet to be partakers of the inheritance of the saints in light."*

"But they that wait upon the Lord shall renew their strength; they shall mount up with wings as eagles; they shall run and not be weary; and they shall walk and not faint." ISAIAH 40:31

"I can do all things through Christ which strengtheneth me." Philippians 4:13 - Please note that ALL THINGS includes our obedience to God, as well as having faith and love, etc.

Let's try to walk together in obedience according to what God is telling each of us. And, if we will listen to Him and allow Him to guide us on this walk through obedience, we will find many rewards along this journey.

Chapter Eight
Journey of Intercession

The word "intercede" means to plead in behalf of one in trouble or to mediate. The word "intercession" means a prayer to God on behalf of another, both of these definitions come from my Webster's Desk Dictionary. If we are to be walking through intercession, going about the business of "interceding" for one another, then, we are to plead in behalf of one who is in trouble. I have found throughout my walk with God that many times I am interceding for someone I have just met or it may be someone I have known a long time that God has brought to my mind whenever I'm praying or reading the Word. Sometimes it is because I have come across that person in my daily walk, maybe at the grocery store, music store, church or some place else. The point I want you to remember is that we ARE to intercede for one another. The way to intercede is to pray to God on behalf of that person. Many times during times of intercession, I may not even know WHO or WHAT I am praying for, only that God has asked me to pray for that person or event. Many times, while praying, it takes the form of speaking in my prayer language (speaking in unknown tongues as the spirit gives utterance) in my prayer closet. (Which is not really a "closet" at all!) We all have different forms of "prayer closets", which is not nearly as important as the fact that you have some place where you are free to intercede, or pray for others. Prayer is no more difficult than conversing with God! Simply talk to God. It doesn't have to be elaborate!

I'm sure that different people who are involved in the ministry of intercession, and make no mistake, it IS a ministry of love, that they have many different methods of modes of worship and prayer. Many times I begin with soothing, uplifting Christian music and before I know it, I am deeply involved in prayer for someone and interceding on their behalf. Sometimes, I go to my prayer closet knowing that someone specific needs to be prayed for and begin to intercede on their behalf, as I know how, and will end up speaking in my prayer language, not even knowing WHAT I am praying about, yet knowing that God knows and this communication with God is being heard by Him and He will take control of the situation in their lives. I may not always know how to pray for someone, so, I usually begin praying God's will over their lives and their situations and God somehow takes over for me, the Holy Spirit begins to actually intercede using my simple prayers. That is an awesome experience, one that anyone who is spirit-filled may experience. I do not understand why we are not more involved in praying for one another. It does lift me up to pray for others and it helps me to get my problems more in perspective sometimes, reminds me that maybe others have problems far worse than mine at times!

There is a popular catch phrase that goes like this: "Prayer Changes Things." I believe that very much. I have even adopted this phrase and taken it to my heart. My journeys throughout life to date have certainly shown this to be true in my life and that of my children. Many times I have seen the results of changes brought about by prayer, in my children, many times throughout their younger lives and on a daily basis! So, why is it that if we KNOW that prayer changes things, we allow prayer to become our last resort when we need help? We, being the humans that we are, think we can do it ourselves, so we try to fix everything first, then, when that doesn't work, we go "limping" to God and cry out to Him, when prayer should have been our "first choice" of action! Prayer should be our first avenue of action. Maybe our wait for the answers wouldn't be as lengthy if we would pray first! See Isaiah 65:24 'And it shall come to pass, that before they call, I will answer; and while they are yet speaking, I will hear."

Wow! To me that means that God has already sent the answer on the way before we even ask! "Ask, and it shall be given you, seek and ye shall find, knock, and it shall be opened unto you; for every one that asketh receiveth; and he that seeketh findeth, and to him that knocketh, it shall be opened." Matthew 7:7,8 If we are interceding for someone else and pleading on their behalf, and God answers that prayer, it is a double reward, because when we pray for someone else, we will also receive a reward, an eternal reward. A friend once told me that every time we do some small kindness for each other, and we are doing it as unto Christ, that we will receive eternal rewards that far outweigh the kindness or act of love that was expressed. We are literally building up our treasures in heaven. That is a bonus and not an incentive to be doing it, because if that is your motivation, then you are not going to build eternal rewards. Isn't it just nice to know that you are busy about the Father's business by (in simple layman's terms) loving one another, by whatever methods are available to us, small kindnesses or acts of love or large monetary gifts or whatever method God has told you to use (maybe intercession), then we are building up eternal rewards.

It is necessary for an Intercessor to have faith. An intercessor must go into that intercession "session" with the knowledge that God is going to do what He has said He will do and that means that He will answer the prayers that are presented by His intercessors on behalf of others. "And all things, whatsoever ye shall ask in prayer, believing, ye shall receive." Matthew 21:22

Do you know that intercessor also means mediator? What does a mediator usually do? A mediator is a person who acts as an agent who goes between two people and gets them to agree on a settlement - in a business situation. I feel that as an intercessor or mediator, sometimes we are required to mediate a situation. To plead on behalf of one person to the Father, to have mercy on them for whatever reasons they may need mercy for!

Sometimes just to pray for someone is to intercede. However, in my experience, I have found that there are different methods of intercession. While praying for a very serious situation and interceding for a friend at one time, I felt the need to dance in the spirit on their behalf. Believe me, that was not something I was used to doing and was not sure that I hadn't really lost my mind. But, when I was obedient to the Holy Spirit and began to dance as an act of intercession on their behalf, God freed some things within me as well as them, and we saw a breakthrough in that situation within a very short time period. There have been other times when I have literally moaned in physical pain for some else's pain while interceding on their behalf. God uses different forms of worship, praise, prayer, dancing, etc., in intercession and I would just like to urge you to be obedient to practice whatever method you feel God is guiding you to use at any given time. I do not dance every time I intercede for someone. There have been times when I had to "be at peace" and be quiet before God after I began to pray for them. God speaks during those quiet times, either to me or to them or TO the situation.

Intercession brings you to a place that you can HEAR God's instructions clearer and you are able to truly "intercede" for whatever the situation is. Sometimes God shares that information with me, other times He doesn't. Sometimes I've interceded for political situations going on either locally or around the world , the church elders, leaders in other areas of life, missionaries, etc.

If you are called to be an Intercessor, and at some point, we all are, because we are to pray for one another, I would encourage you to JUST DO IT! When God has called you to intercede, it is needed AT THAT TIME! You may think that just being one little human being, one person's prayers can't mean that much, but they do, because God takes your prayers and grows them and applies that growth to the situation needing prayer. We are not just in this journey for ourselves! We are the BODY of Christ and each part is dependent on another to survive! It really could be a matter of survival for someone for you to intercede on their behalf at that time.

Isaiah 53:12 makes a strong statement regarding intercession, it says: "Therefore will I divide him a portion with the great, and he shall divide the spoil with the strong; because he hath poured out his soul unto death; and he was numbered with the transgressors; and he bare the sin of many, and made intercession for the transgressors." This verse is referring to the coming Christ - way before Jesus was born - it was a prophetic word about Jesus' coming to earth, showing us that Jesus was the greatest Intercessor of all times. He interceded on our behalf!

Romans 8:26 says: "Likewise the Spirit also helpeth our infirmities; for we know not what we should pray for as we ought; but the Spirit itself maketh intercession for us with groanings which cannot be uttered."

1 Timothy 2:1-6 says: "I exhort therefore, that, first of all, supplications, prayers, intercessions, and giving of thanks be made for all men; for kings, and for all that are in authority; that we may lead a quiet and peaceable life in all godliness and honesty, for this is good and acceptable in the sight of God our Savior, who will have all men to be saved, and to come unto the knowledge of the truth. For there is one God, and one mediator between God and men, the man Christ Jesus; who gave himself a ransom for all, to be testified in due time."

1 Timothy 2:8 also says, "I would therefore that all men pray every where, lifting up holy hands, without wrath and doubting."

Hebrews 7:25 states; "Wherefore he is able also to save them to the uttermost that come unto God by Him, seeing he ever liveth to make intercession for them." This verse follows some verses talking about Jesus in the priesthood. It is His Purpose for living to make intercession for "them" - them being you and I and every person who has walked this earth before us! Wow, we just need to realize that Jesus intercedes for us and if we are going to fashion ourselves after Jesus, which should be our goal, because he is the great intercessor, then we should be interceding for one another as we are called to do.

Sometimes intercessors find that in order to pray for someone, God allows them to acquire a bit of knowledge about a situation or person that they are praying for. I want to encourage you, as an intercessor, to PRAY for that person or situation and not share that information with anyone else, not even to ask a friend to help you pray about the situation (this can become gossip!). The only time I would encourage you to share information is when God has told you to share that information with the person who needs to have something confirmed in their lives. God is not going to tell you to share it with anyone other than the person who you are praying for! Most of the time, you are given that knowledge only to help you PRAY about the situation or person involved. As an intercessor, it is your job to ONLY pray. Many times during intercession, God has shown me things that I am not free to share with anyone else. Those times require tact and diplomacy and I remind myself to ONLY PRAY. If God wants you to release information to anyone, He will tell you. Otherwise, my experience has taught me to stay silent and pray for the people involved.

    Interceding for others can be rewarding and sometimes it can be heart wrenching, but it is a part of our daily walk. Every one of us is called to intercede and to always pray for one another. There are some people, however, whose major calling it is to intercede. That is their gifting and calling. We are all called to intercede and pray as a part of our walk on this journey of faith, love, acceptance of one another. You will notice that it is a lot easier to love one another, too, if we are praying for one another!! What a wonderful journey!

Chapter Nine
Journey of Peace

There is a song we sing in some church services that I've attended throughout the years that goes like this:

> *Peace, Peace, Wonderful Peace,*
> *Coming down from the Father above,*
> *Sweep over my spirit forever, I pray*
> *In fathomless billows of love.*

I would like for you to visualize, if you can, for a moment, what "Peace" looks like!

We think that "peace" means that there are NO problems in our lives, no rifts, it's as smooth as silk, everything is coming up roses, it's rosy! Not so!

Isaiah 26:3 says that God will give us perfect peace if we will keep our mind stayed on Him. "Thou wilt keep him in perfect peace, whose mind is stayed on thee; because he trusteth in thee."

> *"But now in Christ Jesus ye who sometime were far off are made nigh by the Blood of Christ. For He is our peace, who hath made both one, and hath broken down the middle wall of partition between us."* EPHESIANS 2:13,14

"For unto us a child is born, unto us a son is given; and the government shall be upon his shoulder; and his name shall be called Wonderful, Counselor, The Mighty God, The Everlasting Father, The Prince of Peace. Of the increase of his government and peace there shall be no end, upon the throne of David, and upon his kingdom, to order it, and to establish it with judgment and with justice from henceforth even for ever. The zeal of the Lord of hosts will perform this." ISAIAH 9:6, 7

"And the God of Peace shall bruise Satan under your feet shortly. The grace of the Lord Jesus Christ be with you. Amen." ROMANS 16:20

"Lord, thou wilt ordain peace for us, for thou also hast wrought all our works in us." ISAIAH 26:12

"Those things; which ye have both learned, and received, and heard, and seen in me, do; and the God of Peace shall be with you" PHILIPPIANS 4:9

"Therefore being justified by faith, we have peace with God through our Lord Jesus Christ." ROMANS 5:1

"And let the peace of God rule in your hearts, to the which also ye are called in one body; and be ye thankful." COLOSSIANS 3:15

"I will both lay me down in peace, and sleep; for thou, Lord, only makest me dwell in safety." PSALM 4:8

"The Lord will give strength unto His people; the Lord will bless His people with peace." PSALM 29:11

"Peace I leave with you, my peace I give unto you; not as the world giveth, give I unto you. Let not your heart be troubled, neither let it be afraid." JOHN 14:27

> *"Be careful for nothing, but in everything by prayer and supplication with thanksgiving let your requests be made known unto God. And the peace of God, which passeth all understanding, shall keep your hearts and minds through Christ Jesus."* PHILIPPIANS 4:6,7

Peace. What is Peace exactly? The dictionary says it's a state of tranquility or serenity. But, if you have given your heart over to God and you are trying to walk that journey of faith and love, what exactly does peace mean to you, in your daily walk with God? How do we apply it literally to our every day lives? To me, peace means that in the midst of the turmoil, things happening every day in most people's lives, that in the middle of all that "stuff", that God is there and gives me serenity and peace IN THE MIDST OF THE STORM!

If you've ever scrutinized Psalm 23 very much, you will find the verse that says, "He prepares a table before me IN THE MIDST of mine enemies." To be exact, you can locate it in verse 5 and the exact wording in the King James Version states: "Thou prepares a table before me in the presence of mine enemies…". To me, that is the perfect picture of peace, being able to sit down and eat at a table prepared for you that is right in the middle of your enemies! As I told you earlier in this chapter, peace is not exactly what most people picture it to be! Peace is not always having a perfectly untroubled life with no worries and no turmoil. Peace is that thing that allows you to rest assured that God is in control of the situation IN THE MIDST of whatever else is happening! My definition of peace as I have experienced it on this journey is that peace is an assurance that Jesus is interceding for me - I can rely on Him - he's never going to leave me nor forsake me and that I can depend on Him when nobody else can be depended on and HE is my PEACE! Thank God.

In the weekly ministry I am involved in, we have meetings during which prophecy sometimes comes forth and we pray for others. Many times during these meetings, God has led me to "impart peace" to someone for whom I have been led to pray for.

I don't know if these people understand that peace, but I do know that God's peace passes all understanding!

Please refer back to Philippians 4:7 - which says, "And the peace of God, which passeth all understanding, shall keep your hearts and minds through Christ Jesus." I have been told that our "understanding" is in our souls and that when we are saved, it is through the spirit realm, so, therefore, God's spirit imparts peace to our spirits and we are not going to understand it in our souls at times. I have one friend who, when she prays for peace for someone, she refers to this verse quoting, "… the peace that passeth all understanding.". This is one of those things that I would again say, "Just Do It!" Just allow the peace of God to bypass your soul realm and go straight to your spirit and flow throughout your life. Another song that seems to apply here is, "Peace be still, the Father loves you, Peace be still…" What a wonderful part of the journey, to be able to walk in God's peace that passes all understanding!

Chapter Ten
Journey of Purpose

Do you ever wonder what your Purpose in life really is? I have been at a point in my life of asking God, "Look, why am I even here?" "What is it that I am supposed to be doing?" I thought there was some HUGE, big, gigantic thing that I needed to do for God in order to prove my love for Him. Well, in order to find the answer to that question, I really did not have far to search! I found it in John 6:26, 27. My purpose in this life is simply to SERVE GOD! John 6:26 and 27 tells me in Jesus' own words: "Verily, verily, I say unto you, Ye seek me, not because ye saw the miracles, but because ye did eat of the loaves and were filled. Labor not for the meat which perisheth, but for that meat that endureth unto everlasting life, which the Son of Man shall give unto you; for him hath God the Father sealed." and he says in verse 29 of that chapter, "This is the work of God that we believe on him whom he hath sent." Believe in Jesus!

Matthew 6:33 (which is one of my favorite verses in the entire Bible), should also tell us what our purpose on earth is: "But seek ye first the kingdom of God, and his righteousness, and all these things shall be added unto you." Verse 34 goes on to say, "Take no thought for the morrow, for the morrow shall take thought for the things of itself. Sufficient unto the day is the evil thereof." How many times have we been guilty of allowing all the little daily problems to get in the way of us seeking for God and His kingdom? Probably most of us would have to honestly answer that question with an answer of "Most of the time."! It is not God's will for the daily stresses of life to get between us and Him! And, we can know that if we will dedicate time to seeking after Him, all those daily stresses will begin to dim and seem less important, not only that, but He will take care of them for us. Our priority is to seek after God.

I have been known to waste time by continuing to press God for an answer that was already right there before me! I just had to search it out in His Word! For many years, I was guilty of wasting my time and God's during our times together by trying to figure out the small details of what I was "supposed to be doing". What is my gifting? What is my Title? What ministry did I need to be working in?

I am supposed to be involved in the ministry of love! God is love. If I am seeking God first, and God is love, then the most important thing I can be involved in is to love His children. (ALL of them!) The final commandment that Jesus gave to us was to love one another as God loves us! God has loved us in so many ways that we have a very wide variety of ways to chose from, however, loving one another is action, not a description of a feeling! Love is an action verb, not a noun! Love put into action is our purpose on this earth. Seeking God first, knowing that if we do so, all the other things in life will fall into their rightful priority places according to God's will for our lives!

I would like to share with you some verses that have helped me on a daily basis regarding this ministry of love:

>   JAMES 1:19 - *"Be swift to hear, slow to speak, slow to wrath."*

>   PSALM 30:5 - *"For his anger endureth but a moment in His favor is life, weeping may endure for a night, but joy cometh in the morning."* (If God's anger only lasts for a moment - why is it we can allow it to go on for years????)

> II CORINTHIANS 9:8 - *"God is able to make all grace abound toward you; that ye always having all sufficiency in all things, may abound to every good work."*
>
> I JOHN 4:4 - *"Ye are of God, little children, and have overcome them, because greater is He that is in you, than he that is in the world."*
>
> ROMANS 8:31 - *"...if God be for us, who can be against us?"*
>
> NEHEMIAH 8:10 - *"Then he said unto them, Go your way, eat the fat and drink the sweet, and send portions unto them for whom nothing is prepared; for this day is holy unto our Lord; neither be ye sorry, for the joy of the Lord is your strength."*

Again, another song that seems to apply here is:

> *The joy of the Lord is my strength*
> *The joy of the Lord is my strength*
> *The joy of the Lord is my strength!*

Many of us have been given gifts, music, compassion, writing, acting, public speaking, financial abilities, administration, many types of skills and abilities! These, however, are gifts to be used for God's glory, but they are not our PURPOSE! Our purpose is to serve God. We should be using these gifts for God, yes, but they are just that, gifts, not purposes! Sometimes we have a tendency to get our purpose and our talents intertwined in our minds and think that if we are exercising our gifts for God, that we are fulfilling our purpose in life. Not so! It is our responsibility to love one another, to bring others into the family of God. It is our purpose to serve God, using whatever means are available to us!

I just want you to understand that you DO have a purpose for being here! You need to be assured and have peace in your heart that your purpose on earth is to serve God - he made us to serve Him. So, continue on your journey of love with God and walk in your purpose!

Chapter Eleven
Journey of Love

The first question I want to consider throughout this entire chapter is: "Am I in love with Jesus?" What do I really know about love? Love is another one of those words that may mean something other than what you may think it is! Love - God's Love is so big and powerful! Yet, it sometimes requires only a word, a smile, a soft response, a sweet note, a small favor to be expressed.

In a study group that I attend, we have been asked to memorize a part of the "Love Chapter" - 1 Corinthians 13: verses 4-8, which go like this:

*Charity suffered long and is kind; charity envieth not; charity vaunted not
Itself, is not puffed up, doth not behave itself unseemly, seeketh not her
Own, is not easily provoked, thinketh no evil, rejoiceth not in iniquity,
But rejoiceth in the truth; beareth all things, believeth all things; hopeth
All things, endureth all things; charity never faileth;...*

In the Amplified Bible version, these verses read like this:

*Love endures long and is patient and kind; love never is envious nor boils
Over with jealousy; is not boastful or vainglorious, does not display itself
Haughtily, it is not conceited - arrogant and inflated with pride; it is not
Rude (unmannerly) and does not act unbecomingly. Love (God's love
In us) does not insist on its own rights or its own way, for it is not self-
Seeking; it is not touchy or fretful or resentful; it takes no account of the*

*Evil done to it - pays no attention to a suffered wrong. It does not rejoice
At injustice and unrighteousness, but rejoices when right and trust prevail.
Love bears up under anything and everything that comes, is ever ready to
Believe the best of every person, its hopes are fadeless under all
Circumstances and it endures everything (without weakening).
Love never fails -- never fades out or becomes obsolete or comes
To an end.*

These words can become TRUTH to us if we will just take them to heart. Allow God to prove them in our lives! I have to confess to you that God has been having me "re-live" each chapter and walk through some of these things again as they were written! And, in the midst of it all, He has given me peace and a greater love for His people! However, I want to remind us that it is not even about US, it's ALL about HIM! He loves us so very much. Please allow Him to show you how very much He loves you by inviting Him into your heart today. You will never regret it and you WILL BE richly blessed.

When I first began to write this chapter, I actually thought, "What do I know about Love?" I felt that I really knew more about what Love was NOT than what it was! But God reminded me of His love for me and He can be very persistent with that love at times! He has allowed me to experience some different forms of His love the past few months. Some of which surprised me. When I began this chapter, I was actually not feeling very loved by God, so, thought "How can I express God's love to others, when I'm not even feeling it myself right now?" You've probably heard that phrase, "from one extreme to another!" Well, it has been like that in my home lately! I went from having 3 part-time jobs that not one of them would pay a utility bill alone, to several full-time job offers, one of which I did accept. During this month, we had some horrible transportation problems, YET God is our Provider - our Jehova Jirah throughout the entire month. God's love for us has been manifested throughout these months in our lives in ways that only He can do - He allowed different funds to come in to help with our transportation woes. He sent the most unlikely people around to our home to help us out and He sent many friends to help in those times of need - not only financial need, but pastoral, physical, social needs, the whole realm of need - He's been "one step ahead of us" all the way and provided for us before we even knew it sometimes or had time to pray about it!

During this time period, a Bible Study group that I had been attending and come to heavily rely upon, shut down. The couple who held it in their home separated and divorced. I loved attending these meetings and being fed spiritually and socially and came to depend upon these meetings a lot. It was very difficult for me emotionally when it suddenly shut down. And, then, there were three more hurting people to pray for, this couple and their child. So, this goes back to the intercession! Now, I had to intercede for these friends, even though I didn't FEEL like praying for anyone at the time! Guess what! Sometimes God's plans don't fit into our agendas! Bingo! That was my problem! God's timing doesn't always gel with our timing and when WE think things should happen!

Also, during this time, my children were gone to visit with their father for three weeks, three of the longest weeks in my life! However, all of these things brought about a time of intercession, praise and worship that was very sweet and powerful for me. I know that this time brought about a more peaceful and powerful prayer life for me and it gave me more security in God's love for me! Amazing the way God works! God used flowers, books, music, pictures and a lot of different things to enrich my life. He cared enough about me and the small details in my life. He loves you just like that, too! We are each individually made and so different, yet, He knows just exactly what it takes to reach each one of us wherever we are at!

Several weeks ago, I had an "encounter" with one of my children and told them "If I didn't love you so much, I just wouldn't care how you acted or what you did!" We were in the middle of a heated discussion. It made me stop and think about our relationships with God at times. We get ourselves into some pretty unpleasant situations (or trouble) and God has to remind us that He still loves us no matter what we have done! I find it important to remind my children of my love for them whenever it is necessary to discipline them. It's like that with God, too, he loves us so much, irregardless of what we may have done or how far off the path we may have wandered. A song I love to listen to refers to this in its words: "God still loves you no matter what you've done or how hard you've shut the door.!" Wow! I like that! Doesn't that just tell you that He's there for you all the time and will be in the future? He is not going to desert you just because of something you have done wrong or because of your sins, either secret or public. Guilt and condemnation are not a part of God's plan for your life! Forgiveness and His love are! He wants to forgive you and to love you, allowing you to grow and go forward in His will for your life.

If you have trouble discerning what God's will for your life is, just remember that He created each of us to praise Him. If you don't have a clue what your "talents or gifts" are (abilities) - JUST DO IT! Live your life as if to praise God with everything you do - and you'll find your way onto the right path with Him. Maybe that sounds unrealistic to you, but I always try to do whatever tasks are at hand as if I am doing them for God and do my very best. That's all I'm recommending that you do. If you know you have certain abilities and talents, then, use them for God.

I remember one time when I was married and lived in San Antonio with my two younger children and a non-believing non-Christian husband who did NOT work, and I was in a position that if I didn't work, my family would have been literally living on the streets. I was supporting my children and a husband out of necessity. I tried to maintain an attitude of doing it as unto God, to please God by doing my best and God continued to bless us. At that time, I became very discouraged with my life - hopelessness and despair were a daily part of my life then, and I asked God to get me out of this horribly abusive relationship. I knew I could no longer live with fear for my life and my children's lives and in fear of what was going to happen when I came home from working 10-12 hours a day. I was ready to give it all up! That is exactly what God wanted me to do. To turn to Him and give it all to Him. Which I did.

God's love for me was so great that He took this man completely out of our home and spared my life and that of my children. You cannot imagine the release that came into our home with the removal of the abuse and pornography he participated in, along with the spirits attached to those lifestyles. God loves us so much that we have not had to see this man again. God gave us back peace and joy and kept us throughout that time.

It's all about God's Love for us, friend, it really is. And, He wants to have a very personal, loving two-way relationship with each one of us. It takes two to maintain a relationship - us and God! God loves you just as much as He loves me! He doesn't love any one of us more than another. Remember, He is no respecter of persons! You can know this in your heart and mind if you are committed to God and to living for Him, it's there in His Word for you, how much He loves you! God sent His Son, Jesus Christ, to die a very horrible death on the cross for us, me and you, so that we might be able to have a one-on-one relationship with God, a direct line to God is ours! He loves you that much and whether you are male or female, He wants to hold you in His arms and become intimate with you and love you. He's made it so easy for us!

Our only requirement is to accept Him into our hearts, repent (turn from your carnal or worldly ways - stop doing those things you know are not right) and to follow Jesus! He promised to make us fishers of men. Please don't tell me you thought he was just talking to the disciples and that was ancient history! It is NOT! It's for us today.

God loves you so much that He knows every atom in your body. He knows every hair on your head. The Bible says if He cares enough to take care of the birds of the air, how much more He loves you and that if you will seek Him first and not "sweat the everyday details of life, or the small stuff", (this is paraphrased a la Rhonda) that all those other things will be taken care of. Actually, this verse is found in Matthew 6:33 and it reads like this: "Seek ye first the Kingdom of God and His righteousness and all these things shall be added unto you." The next verse says, "Take therefore no thought for the morrow for the morrow shall take thought for the things of itself." He loves us so much that He doesn't want us to waste our time worrying about things - He wants to be intimately involved in a relationship with you wherein you forget everything else and concentrate on Him. (One way to look at the word intimate is INTO ME HE SEES!) God wants you to pray, to talk to Him, to give Him praise, to worship Him. He wants your most costly commodity, time! He wants to spend time with you no matter what activities you are involved throughout your days. All He really wants is YOU. He loves you that much! I know from experience that a man or woman will tell you that they love and will always be there for you and no matter how much they mean it at the time, that it just is not possible for any one person to be there whenever you need them every time! God's love is pure and God is ALWAYS there for you no matter what else is happening! He created you so that He could share His love with you and He really is not "into" having your worries take the place of your time with Him.

The Bible is God's Word for you and it is God's love story for you, too. I encourage you to get into it and read it, savor it every chance you get. Not necessarily to make it a "ritual", even though a good ritual would be better than a bad one, but, read it and apply it to your life. Remember, everything you need to help you in your life is there in the Bible, in God's love letters to you. Just like when we humans enjoy getting letters of praise or love letters, it is the same thing! The difference is that God's love is pure and honest and always there for you. His love encompasses you like no other can. The Bible demonstrates to us God's love for us, including discipline. (Surely as a parent, some of you can relate to that!) We are HIS children and He loves us even more than we can imagine. After all, we only have finite minds - God's love is infinite, cannot be measured and never ends. Each one of us is loved with ALL His love. It's not just there for one select person and not another, and it is not dependent on anything you can do for Him. He does not love one child more than another. His love may be expressed to each one of us in different methods, because we are individuals, we are different and we respond to different things. I have a different history with God than you, so, He may chose a different method in dealing with me than he would with you. Each person's history with God is different from one another, features, physical, emotions, spiritual experiences, not better or worse, just different. I truly believe that God sees us wherever we are at and loves us whatever our status in life. Don't think that because of something you may or may not have done that God is going to love you any less! NOTHING can separate us from the love of God. He loves you   REGARDLESS of where you're at and it's expressed in his love letter to you. His Word.

When Jesus was asked in the course of his teachings what the greatest commandment was, it was his response that "LOVE" was the greatest commandment of all. He commanded that we love God above all else and that we love one another and his FINAL command to us is that we are to love one another as Christ has loved the Church. (The Church being the body of Christ - you and I, God's children) Jesus loved the "church" so much that he gave up the wonderful, glorious life that was His and came and walked on this earth. He performed miracles, taught anyone who would listen to Him how to love God and then He died on the cross for us. What's love? If that isn't love, then we don't have a clue! God Knows. And, He's willing to share His love with us. What more could we ask for? Nothing, because that's the ultimate - to have God's love. Now, I have shared with you in this book that sometimes it is not easy and sometimes it requires a lot of soul searching and forgiveness, thinking of someone else instead of ourselves at times and sometimes it even requires some "stretching" on our part! I've been "stretched" some during the writing of this book, through some of the people God has led us to during the past several months. Some of these people have waltzed into our lives for short times and are already gone and others remain today. Some things that have happened we don't understand, but, we pray that any contact with us has helped to draw them to Christ, to salvation.

It is the prayer of my children and myself that anyone who reads this book will be led to come to Jesus, accept Him into their hearts and if that has already happened in their lives, that their lives will somehow be enhanced and lifted up through our testimony on these pages. Please remember that no matter what part of the path on this journey that you are traveling on, that first and foremost, GOD LOVES YOU! He loves you even if you are blatantly sinning every step of the way. He STILL loves you.

I told you at the beginning of this book that journeys can be fun and I intentionally did not mention those things that could be pitfalls or cause fear because we all seem to have enough of that in our lives. I wanted to encourage you and pray that God instills His peace, love, joy, and all the fruits of His Spirit into your hearts on a daily basis. Fear has no part with love or joy. And, fear is the enemy of faith. I hope that this short journey we have taken together has instilled excitement in you to read your Bible and pray and learn to depend on God for every phase of your life. And, I pray that traversing these pages has helped you to understand just how HUGE God's love for you is! He loves you with HIS WHOLE HEART - He desires you and He is pursuing (wooing) you. It is the best relationship you will ever experience. He loves and loves and loves and never stops!

TAKE A JOURNEY INTO GOD'S LOVE.

I love you with the love of God.

Rhonda

Printed in the United States
76251LV00006B/121-168